G000143862

A NEW DEAL FOR SOCIAL WELFARE

Are we creating a cash-register society?

Social workers have become case managers.

Local authorities increasingly buy and sell welfare services.

It's the contract culture: Social Services in the market-place.

Bob Holman, former Professor of Social Administration at the University of Bath, has been a social worker for over 20 years. He regularly contributes to professional journals, *The Guardian* and other national newspapers. And he lives on a large, mainly council, housing scheme in Glasgow amongst people who have been branded as 'the underclass'.

This book is a powerful analysis of the theories which have transformed social welfare from being a 'caring profession' to a buying-and-selling business. It is also a passionate plea for welfare to adopt new principles and practices.

A
NEW DEAL
FOR SOCIAL
WELFARE

Bob Holman

A LION BOOK

Copyright © 1993 Bob Holman

The author asserts the moral right
to be identified as the author of this work

Published by
Lion Publishing plc
Sandy Lane West, Oxford, England
ISBN 0 7459 2848 X

First edition 1993

All rights reserved

A catalogue record for this book is available
from the British Library

Printed and bound in Great Britain
by Cox & Wyman Ltd, Reading

Contents

1

The New Right and Social Welfare

During my lifetime, I have witnessed enormous changes in the Social Services in Britain. When I was born in the 1930s, the influence of the Poor Law still held sway. I can recall my grandmother's fear, 'Don't let me finish in the Union' (the workhouse). Following the Second World War, Labour's landslide victory led to the modern welfare state with the National Health Service, Family Allowances, National Assistance and, within local authorities, the Children's Departments. We rejoiced at the noble words of the National Assistance Act, 'The existing Poor Law shall cease to have effect.'

Personally I gained by proceeding to free education at a grammar school and then university. My sister, who had passed the eleven-plus examination some years before, missed out. The new services were based on the premise that the state, not private firms or charity, had the responsibility for the well-being of its citizens. Welfare, education and health needs were to be met regardless of ability to pay.

Nearly forty years on, another transformation has taken place. Under Margaret Thatcher and then John Major as Prime Ministers, Conservative Governments have put into practice the ideology of what is known as the New Right. Its impact has been deep and extensive, touching private enterprise, public services, fiscal and monetary policy. New Right policies have also influenced social welfare, the personal social services and social workers. My analysis and interpretation is that the impact has been an adverse one. In this book, I will:

critically examine the New Right's doctrines and policies;

consider the influence of the New Right on social welfare;

suggest mutuality as an alternative basis.

The New Right

The New Right has not lacked persuasive exponents. Hayek, Seldon, Lees, Harris, Griffiths, have poured out publications, often through the right-wing pressure group, the Institute of Economic Affairs. Of all the gurus, the greatest popularizer of New Right ideas has been Milton Friedman, although he prefers the term 'liberal' which, he says, in the nineteenth century meant 'the doctrines pertaining to a free man'.[1] The New Right title emerged in Britain as its supporters turned the Conservative Party in a new direction.

In his influential book *Capitalism and Freedom*, Friedman identifies two foundations to freedom. One is that 'the scope of government must be limited', the other that 'power must be dispersed'.[2] Few, certainly not the present writer, would argue with that. However, Friedman looks upon most government activity as undesirable and would like it limited to the conduct of foreign policy, upholding law and order, arranging monetary budgetary policies and, in general, acting as an 'umpire' to see that the rules of the game are observed. For these ends, government would require some income to be obtained by a low 'flat-rate' tax.[3]

Outside these functions, society should be run by the competitive or free market which Friedman and his followers regard as the means both of limiting government and dispersing power. The free market is one which, almost untrammelled by legislation, allows the laws of supply and demand to operate, whether it concerns small firms providing for individual consumers or millionaire speculators bidding for control of multi-national companies. Private, not state-owned enterprises are to dominate. Even in activities such as education, in which Friedman concedes the state might take some initiative, any provision should not be direct, but should be in the form of vouchers to parents, so that they could trade in a market made up of schools run for financial profit.

The competitive system works, the New Right writers agree, because all individuals are driven by self-interest. Lord Harris explains that we must accept that greed is 'the reality' of people's behaviour, and approvingly cites Adam

Smith's famous dictum, 'It is not from the benevolence of the butcher, the brewer or the baker that we expect our dinner, but from their regard for their own interest.'[4] The free market allows full rein to self-interest which therefore maximizes the creation of resources. It also allows full rein to individualism; Friedman adds that 'the individual [is] the ultimate entity in society', with the free market or capitalism the means of 'enlarging the role of the individual'.[5] Human beings are therefore regarded as individualistic and materialistic. Obligations towards non-relatives, neighbours, society, play little part in New Right philosophy. Indeed, Margaret Thatcher declared that there was no such thing as society, only individuals.

A free market, unhindered by government and allowing private companies and private individuals to pursue their own ends, results in three major benefits, according to New Right writers.

The first benefit is greater freedom and democracy. In the capitalist market, the consumer is free to buy what he or she likes. This economic freedom, Friedman argues, is also a political one, for it gives citizens a freedom of choice which is denied to members of totalitarian regimes. By contrast, Friedman cites the example of government legislation which compels people to contribute towards their old-age pensions. This is a reduction of economic and political liberty. He writes,

'Those of us who believe in freedom must believe also in the freedom of individuals to make their own mistakes. If a man knowingly prefers . . . to use his resources for current enjoyment, deliberately choosing a penurious old age, by what right do we prevent him doing so?'[6]

If individuals and firms can buy, sell and negotiate as they like, then they are economically and politically free. The market gives choice and it is choice which, according to Friedman, is the basis of democracy.

The second benefit is efficiency. New Right pundits scorn central and local government agencies as overstaffed, wasteful and inefficient. Public or state involvement in human activities, Friedman declares, 'has given birth to a large bureaucracy that shows tendencies of growing by what it feeds on, by extending its scope from one area of life to another'.[7] By contrast, companies which operate within competitive markets and which are solely concerned with making profit are seen as streamlined and efficient.

The third benefit of a free market is economic growth. The greater capacity of private firms to produce and sell goods, the New Right claims, then leads to the greater accumulation of wealth, investment and employment. Their leading figures attributed Britain's slow economic growth rate in the 1960s and 1970s to the willingness of both Labour and Conservative Governments to increase state expenditure. Their solution was to put nearly all activities, even welfare ones, into the private market. As Arthur Seldon recommended, 'National economic expansion can best be helped by putting welfare by stages into the market where the consumer will rule instead of the politician.'[8]

The free market inevitably leads to vast disparities in the distribution of goods, incomes and wealth. This inequality is welcomed by the New Right on the grounds that it is the prospect of personal gain and the fear of poverty that drive people to work hard in the present and to save for the future. Indeed, Friedman claims that 'equality comes sharply into conflict with freedom; one must choose. One cannot be both an egalitarian, in this sense, and a liberal.'[9]

What is the attitude of the New Right to citizens left in poverty as the result of the free market? The writings of its leading advocates are hardly characterized by compassion. In a context in which values are shaped by economic factors, the poor are seen to deserve their fate either because they lack the abilities to compete or because they are lazy. Margaret Thatcher, the foremost New Right politician, claimed that the economic transformation her policies brought to the country would eventually 'trickle down' and so benefit even the poorest.

However, most agree that the latter cannot be left entirely destitute. Friedman believes that 'One recourse, and in many ways the most desirable, is private charity'.[10] Failing that, the state should provide what he calls 'a floor' or safety net. However, he makes it clear that this should be kept to a minimum for fear that state bureaucracy would then grow, so leading to higher taxes which would inhibit others from being industrious.

Similarly, Friedman and his like are agreed that the state must intervene to protect children from neglect and abuse. Again, this objective springs not so much from compassion for children but from the understanding that children are 'consumer goods' who will one day contribute to the market.[11] Such protection is to be achieved not by costly facilities to support parents in their tasks but rather by prosecutions, threats of removal, and, in the end, actual removal of children from their families.

The Impact of the New Right

New Right supporters have had the satisfaction of seeing British Governments, since 1979, dedicated to the implementation of their proposals. State industries have been sold off to the private sector. Financial encouragement has been given to private welfare, especially pensions, medicine and residential care. The introduction of and pressure for hospital trusts, fund-holding general practices and opted-out schools has created internal markets within health and education. The extent of local government has been restricted by legislation to cut its powers and finances and by forcing it to contract out for many services. In 1978–79, local authorities raised 57 per cent of their own income, mainly via local business and property taxes. Changes imposed from on high mean that they now raise only 18 per cent and so are heavily dependent on central government grants, which come with rigid conditions. Simultaneously, central government expenditure has been checked by not allowing some benefits, especially Child Benefit, to be upgraded with inflation; by the virtual abolition of Single Payment Grants for essential items such as cookers for people dependent on Income Support; by the removal of any Income Support, except in rare cases, for unemployed 16–17 year olds; and by reduced levels for those aged 18–25 years.

Money saved in these ways has been reallocated in the form of income tax cuts so that since 1979 the highest paid 10 per cent of the population has gained more than £50,000 million. Not least, the removal of much wage protection and work protection legislation has enabled employers to reduce the wages of the lowest paid in the expectation that the firms' greater profitability would lead to more wealth, investment and jobs.

The impact of the New Right has also been evidenced in the popularization of a theory to explain continuing unemployment, poverty and other social malaises. This 'underclass' explanation has been associated with an American, Charles Murray, whose work has been published in Britain by the Institute of Economic Affairs. His views have been taken up by academics such as Ralf Dahrendorf and David Green, by journalists such as Matthew Parris, and by politicians such as Michael Heseltine and David Willetts. They identify a rapidly growing and evil underclass whose attitudes and behaviour are quite distinct from the rest of the population. Murray claims its membership comes from two sources, from 'young, healthy, low income males [who] choose not to take jobs' and from single mothers who choose to have children outside stable relationships.[12] The bored men turn to drugs and crime. The feckless women, it is claimed, neglect their children who thus become the next generation of delinquent layabouts. Both groups promote unemployment and poverty. Further, the underclass is increasing so rapidly—according to Parris it makes up three-quarters of some council estates[13]—that it threatens the virtues of hard work and marriage. Ralph Dahrendorf says, 'the underclass is the living doubt in the prevailing values which will eat into the texture of the societies in which we are living'.[14]

And what is to blame for the underclass? State welfare which allows young men to be idle and encourages young women to have babies knowing that local authorities will fit them out with council flats. Just as Friedman blames public services for the slow-down of the economy, so his followers blame them for continuing social malaises. In order to counter the underclass, they recommend:

cutting welfare support so that young people are forced to compete in the job market for their incomes; and

condemning its members so that they are shamed into different behaviour.

Digby Anderson proposes that the right to vote be removed from the long-term unemployed.[15] At the Conservative Conference in 1992, the Social Security minister, Peter Lilley, mocked lone mothers by singing of them as 'young ladies who get pregnant just to jump the housing list'. Murray states, 'I want to reintroduce the notion of blame.'[16] Public condemnation, it is claimed, would enable the underclass to be controlled.

Thus by the 1990s the New Right analysis was complete. Its economic experts had identified the reasons for Britain's ailing economy and suggested the cure. Its social experts then devised an explanation for any failures—the underclass. The solutions for both the economic and the social ills were the same—privatize as much human activity as possible, encourage the pursuit of personal gain, reduce public expenditure to a minimum, and make life even harder for the poor.

A Local Critique

It would be churlish to ignore the positive contribution of New Right advocates. Their criticisms of the waste and bureaucracy within the government's civil service have been justified. Some of the reorganizations planned on being carried through may well be beneficial. They have had the courage to attack the power of the legal and medical professions. One pamphlet even suggested privatizing the monarchy. They have constantly railed against the curtailment of individual liberties in communist countries. None the less, I will argue that their analysis is often faulty and their practices little short of disastrous.

I will criticize the New Right from two levels, the local and the general. I live and work in Easterhouse which Murray cites as one of the classical domains of the underclass of those 'communities without fathers [where] the kids tend to run wild'.[17] I will consider the effect of the New Right policies on Easterhouse and whether the underclass explanation stands up to examination.

Easterhouse is a peripheral Glasgow estate built during the 1950s. At one time its population totalled 60,000 with the vast majority living in council accommodation. Much of the housing was in tenement flats, yet most new residents welcomed the move from the inner city slums to modern buildings which had indoor toilets, baths and, in some cases, gardens. Further jobs were fairly plentiful so that even in 1971 nearly 90 per cent of economically active males were in employment. From the late 1970s, however, unemployment rose steeply. Residents suffered from city-wide closures in the shipbuilding, iron, steel and coal industries and from local closures in manufacturing plants. The Strathclyde Region and Glasgow District Council had also been prominent employers yet, faced with government restrictions, they too had to shed staff.

The New Right analysis has been that the contraction of state-subsidized industries such as shipbuilding and the reduction of local government employment would free the competitive market. Places such as Easterhouse should have benefited in two ways: first, by the arrival of private companies eager to take advantage of a large pool of labour willing to accept low wages; second, by the 'trickle down' effect in that as the nation as a whole prospered so places like Easterhouse would also benefit.

Neither prediction has been fulfilled. Far from improving, unemployment has multiplied. By the early 1990s, the unemployment rate was over 30 per cent with even this figure excluding anyone under 18, those on job schemes, women with children who wanted to work, and certain other categories who desired a job but were not registered as unemployed. Further, the trickle has not even been a drop. The economy of Easterhouse is still such that its large population lacks a major bank, a cinema, a petrol station.

Another strong plank in New Right policy has been to reduce welfare spending and benefits, both to drive feather-bedded residents into jobs and to encourage charities to do more. The social security cuts have occurred, the market has been freed, yet few Easterhouse citizens have found new jobs or clawed their way out of poverty. Today 64 per cent of Easterhouse schoolchildren are in receipt of school clothing grants—that is they come from families with very low incomes. Certainly, some charities have tried to respond to the increase in social suffering. I live close to the Salvation Army where the gallant captain has opened a huge furniture store. In one week, he distributed 41 second-hand beds and, with stocks exhausted, was giving out mattresses for children to sleep on. Apart from the point that families in desperate need should not have to make do with second-hand goods, the fact is that charities lack the resources to cope with the increased demands made upon them. New Right welfare policy has been a failure.

New Right authors constantly play the notion of individual freedom as their trump card. They claim that in a free market economy individuals can choose their jobs, can choose how to spend their money, can choose whether to save or not: they are free.

Yet consider these Easterhouse examples. A neighbour of mine earns £1.90 an hour for a 72-hour week. Even with Child Benefit she struggles to feed her family and furnish the home: she has no freedom to invest in a private pension for her old age.

A couple with two children have £105 a week for their family. From this they are having £10 a week deducted to pay for a Social Fund Loan to buy a cooker. The father cannot find a job despite constant applications. They cannot afford a holiday. They cannot buy a car to widen their choices.

Another friend, observing that I was going to a conference in London, said, 'It's all right for you, I'm a prisoner in Easterhouse.' He could not move out. He could not even pay the fare to visit relatives in London. He has no freedom of choice.

Another neighbour is a cleaner in a service which was privatized: she was then offered just part-time work, with reduced work benefits, fewer holidays and much lower pay. She concluded that she had no choice but to accept.

The trouble with the New Right is that they view the free market from their own positions as secure, affluent, middle-class professionals. Friedman says, 'If I do not like what my local community does, be it in sewage disposal, or zoning, or schools, I can move . . .' [18] Similarly, he says that in the free market he has the freedom to choose whether to put his money in secure stocks or risk speculation on the stock exchange. But these freedoms depend upon the prior advantage of having jobs, opportunities, savings. The market provides freedom for the privileged. And the changes made under the New Right in Britain have done nothing to improve the lot of the deprived and hence have done nothing to improve their freedoms. If all people are to participate in the freedom of the market economy then resources would have to be much more equally distributed. Yet Friedman says this should never happen for freedom and equality are incompatible. The reality in places such as Easterhouse is that New Right policies have widened inequalities and so destroyed liberties.

Not least, Easterhouse demonstrates the inadequacy of the underclass explanation. Despite rising unemployment, the majority of males remain in work even though it is often low-paid work, part-time jobs or work schemes. In short, Easterhouse is not characterized by young men who choose not to work. Further, 72 per cent of Easterhouse children are within two-parent families. And most lone parents soon marry or cohabit. In terms of willingness to work and wanting stable family lives, its residents hold similar views to the rest of the population.

This is not to say that crime and drug abuse are not problems. It is to say that unemployment and poverty and other social malaises should not be attributed to young people developing wrong values from a feather-bedding welfare state. Rather the deprivations are imposed upon people by government policies and economic forces beyond their control. The underclass thesis should be seen less as an explanation of the state of places like Easterhouse and more as a New Right excuse which diverts blame away from the dire results of New Right practices.

The deductions drawn from my experience in one estate can be applied more widely. New Right policies, far from solving Britain's difficulties, have led to an intensification of unemployment and poverty. Reductions in state expenditure have failed to push Income Support recipients into jobs because the free market has not reacted in ways the New Right predicted. National surveys, for instance those drawn upon by Anthony Heath, reveal that welfare recipients are, if anything, more motivated to work and more pro-child and family than the rest of the population. In other words, there is no underclass.[19] New Right analysis, policies and explanations have been found wanting.

A General Critique

New Right theories and recommendations go far beyond local communities. They make far-ranging claims about the merits of capitalism and the defects of collective action. Yet these claims are based on assumptions which do not stand up to examination.

For a start, New Right apologists tend to assume thatstate services are inherently evil. The welfare state is blamed for promoting the underclass. Local authority services are dismissed as inefficient. Consequently, over the last 15 years, public services have been privatized and local authorities' powers curtailed. Yet Kirk Mann, in the midst of a devastating attack on Murray's scholarship, points out that the social evils which Murray attributes to state welfare services flourished to a greater extent in Victorian times before public services were known.[20] Many statutory services have been an undoubted success. Local authorities ensured the supply of pure and cheap water. Council housing may now be in decline and under-funded but it provided hundreds of thousands of adequate dwellings for citizens who had been confined to privately rented slums. Even Friedman concedes that state-financed roads, dams, space research and public health measures have been cost-effective and highly successful.[21] Of course, public services are not always efficient and reliable. But there is no intrinsic reason why they are inferior to privately-run services.

The New Right also assumes that private enterprise promotes democracy. Friedman even claims that it was the free market system which enabled black people to overcome discrimination in the USA and overlooks the part played by state legislation.[22] No doubt, within totalitarian Soviet regimes the emergence of private enterprise did constitute an alternative voice to the state. But one of the failings of New Right authors, particularly Friedman and Hayek, is to contrast the virtues of capitalism with the vices of communism and then assume the vices also apply to countries which have been influenced by democratic socialism.[23]

This one-sided focus ignores the fact that the growth of private enterprise power can also undermine democracy. As early as 1959, Richard Titmuss identified the enormous assets of building societies, pension and insurance companies. In his aptly titled lecture 'The Irresponsible Society', he explained that the monetary decisions of such institutions were affecting millions of people yet were being made by a small minority over whom shareholders, let alone the public at large, had no real influence. Undemocratic.

Today the same private bodies possess even greater holdings. Particularly important is the growth of pension funds which are invested in ways beyond the knowledge let alone the consent of the individuals to whom they really belong. Building societies may award enormous salaries to top officials—while making lower staff redundant—without any meaningful permission from individuals who place their savings with them.

Further, the advances of information technology (IT) mean that monies can be shifted rapidly between economies. On Black Wednesday, when the Government tried unsuccessfully to defend sterling in the Exchange Rate Mechanism, a minority of free market speculators were able to take £8 billion out of the British economy with the population powerless to act.

Again, the concentration of economic power into a few hands, which results from unfettered capitalism, means that the ownership of newspapers and other media forms are restricted to a minority. Undemocratic. As Titmuss argued, the preservation of democracy now requires 'public ownership, public responsibility, and public accountability'.[24]

Not least, the New Right pundits assume that competition always leads to greater efficiency. Perhaps they have never been responsible for their own cars. Anyone who has dealt with the garages of large private companies will be familiar with their frequent over-charging, slackness, rudeness and dangerous inefficiency. Similarly, national banks are often highly inefficient. Competition is not a panacea. Private companies operating within the free market system are not free of excessive bureaucracy. A relative of mine who held a managerial position in ICI was driven to despair by its red tape. Consider changes within the Health Service now that the Government has enforced internal, competitive markets. Between 1989 and 1991, the National Health Service in England took on an extra 18,110 managerial and administrative staff while cutting 8,450 nursing positions. Inefficiency is not the prerogative of statutory organizations and it is not necessarily lessened by market forces.

In fact, greater efficiency is not the whole of the New Right case for privatization. For instance, the British postal services have made huge profits without government subsidies and are acknowledged as probably the most efficient in the world. Yet the present Government has still decreed that they will be privatized. The reasons appear to be that the Government requires money in order to stop raising taxes and that the sell-off will allow private individuals to pocket the enormous profits. The prospect of individual gain, in short, greed, is the driving force behind New Right policies. The free market allows full play to human selfishness and, as a result, a greed which shows little concern for the effect on others now dominates British business ethics and, increasingly, personal values.

The dominance of greed is seen amongst directors of private enterprises who, at a time of national recession and cuts in incomes for lower staff, award themselves huge salary increases. Thus the company Ultramor distributed £6.7 million between its seven directors. It is seen in a decline in integrity with, for instance, some drug firms concealing the terrible side effects of drugs because they were yielding enormous profits. It is seen in politics where MPs who legislate for the privatization of public utilities subsequently obtain lucrative directorships or consultancies with the new bodies. It is seen in the City where the lust for money has prompted an escalation of company fraud.

It is even seen in those who once proclaimed high ideals. During the late sixties and early seventies I mixed with a number of community activists and young academics who voiced beliefs in greater equality, in living in deprived areas, in rejecting high salaries and positions of power in favour of others. One of my saddest experiences has been to observe their noble intentions slowly fade. Today some of the erstwhile radicals are prepared to pocket £50,000 or more in salary, to live in luxury, to distance themselves from poor people—and all in a society where thousands dwell in poverty in damp homes and cannot even afford a weekend holiday away. They have abandoned their early principles in favour of the new morality. Nothing more vividly displays the pervasive grip which New Right values now have on British society.

And what of those poor dwellers in damp homes? The New Right has little time and less compassion for them. In their devastating critique of western culture, Michael Schluter and David Lee explain that the rise of individualism is accompanied by the decline of obligation. The New Right claims it has freed individuals, but it has freed them to worship the god of Mammon. Consequently, successful individuals feel few obligations towards others (apart from relatives) and oppose the spending of 'their' money on collective services. Yet, as Schluter and Lee point out, by weakening social obligation they also weaken social cohesion and create a more uncaring and more irresponsible nation.[25]

To sum up: New Right policies have failed to revive the economy. On the contrary, they have slowed the growth rate, lengthened the dole queues and deepened poverty. By exalting the free market and private ownership they have, despite their claims, restricted the choices of many and weakened democracy. Above all, they have made a god out of Mammon so that personal gain and material selfishness are regarded as virtues while the compassion for the disadvantaged and a readiness to share goods and power are sneered at as weaknesses.

2

The Contract Culture

My major concern is with the personal social services. The Barclay Report defines them as 'those services for which local authority Social Services committees have responsibility and similar services provided by voluntary organizations'. It makes clear that these are services which help families with dependent children, elderly people, mentally and physically disabled people, and certain individuals with difficulties such as drug abuse.[26] The personal social services are usually associated with social workers yet they also employ home helps, care assistants, family aides and many other kinds of staff whom the Barclay Report described as social service workers. The actual activity carried out by the services is often referred to as social welfare.

Why has a book about the personal social services spent several pages examining the New Right? The reason is that New Right values, explanations, policies and practices are now permeating these services—though they are often unrecognized. It has been necessary to explain the failings and dangers of the New Right in order to shed light on what is happening and what could happen to social welfare.

The New Right influence on the personal social services has been exerted in three ways: by legislation, by restrictions on local authority budgets and by the emphasis on private-enterprise management. First, influence has been exerted by legislation, in particular the National Health Service and Community Care Act (1990) which was implemented in 1993. This Act not only transferred much responsibility from the Health Service to the Social Services for care in the community but also determined the ways and procedures through which Social Service Departments (SSDs) and Social Work Departments (SWDs), as they are called in Scotland, deal with elderly, disabled and handicapped people (now more frequently referred to as people with special needs).

In the White Paper *Caring For People*, which preceded the Act, the Government, in classic New Right terminology, stated, 'Promoting choice and independence underlies all the Government's proposals' and that they wanted to 'give people a greater individual say in how they live their lives'.[27] It added that people should not be left unnecessarily to live in hospitals or other large institutions but should have freedom to decide on how they lived in the community. Few, if any, will disagree with that. It continued that the means of achieving this end was less through direct local authority provision and more through 'a mixed economy of welfare'. The resulting legislation made it clear

28

that local authorities had a duty to assess the needs of users and to meet them through what are frequently called internal and external markets. The former are where a SSD may make a contract with a service within its own agency, the latter where it places one with an outside body which has submitted a tender.

In practice, many SSDs have split themselves into purchasing and providing sections, with the purchasers seeking the best bargains for, say, residential care for the elderly or meals on wheels for the housebound. However, the Government's wish to favour the 'independent' sector, that is, voluntary or private-enterprise agencies, was made clear when it specified that 85 per cent of the £539 million transferred to local authorities for community care in 1993/4 had to be spent with this sector.

So far, the Government has not legislated that SSDs must contract out its work with families and children, although some have begun to do so in regard to adoption and fostering placements, day nurseries, the running of centres for alleged child abusers, the overseeing of child protection cases and the supervising of the after-care of children who are the responsibility of local authorities. Moreover, at a 1993 conference entitled 'Child Care and the Contract Culture', the Government minister Tim Yeo stated, 'Local authorities and the independent providers have much to gain from a whole-hearted embracing of the contract culture'. The Government then established a Support Force for residential child care with a particular brief, to make use of the private sector. Clearly, the Government is giving the green light for the welfare of children to be put out to tender.

The second way New Right influence is exerted is by stiff restrictions on local authority budgets. Central to New Right belief is that statutory spending must be cut. Accordingly, since 1979, changes in the Rate Support Grant mechanisms have limited the amounts local authorities receive from central governments; the introduction of the infamous Community Charge (since abolished) limited what could be raised locally; and the imposition of rate-capping limited their expenditure on services. Not surprisingly, in 1993 the Association of Directors of Social Services in England announced that four-fifths of SSDs were having to plan cuts in services while its counterparts in Scotland revealed that their budgets provided less than half enough to restore and update the buildings they used. The New Right had succeeded in restraining local government expenditure on welfare even though legislation was placing greater demands upon it.

The third way influence is exerted is by the repeated message that Social Services require the methods, techniques, approaches and values of private-enterprise managers. Some personal services agencies began to appoint top staff from managers without social work qualifications. Some—certainly not all—sent their staff on management training courses where they absorbed the New Right management culture in which managers are macho controllers fuelled less by welfare altruism and more by personal gain. As the secretary of the ADSS put it, 'There are directors who will say that it is a managerial job, that running a department is no different from running a string of garages or a supermarket chain.' [28]

The New Right has been by no means the only influence on the personal social services in recent years. But, as in the rest of society, it has been a pervasive one. Legislation to impose internal and external markets, the sharp restrictions on statutory spending, the doctrine of management supremacy plus, it must be added, the underclass dogma which condemns many of the users of the services, have combined to mould the environment, values and practices of social welfare. In my judgment, the outcomes are—or are likely to be—serious, adverse and regrettable in the following ways.

Managerial Social Work

The personal social services have always required efficient management. I used to work for the former local authority Children's Departments. They too had to operate within set budgets. There was never a bottomless pit of cash. Today the duties and budgets of the personal social services are far more extensive and complex, but the task of management should still be the same, to enable social workers and other staff to do their jobs properly, with individuals and groups, within a context of social work methods and values.

Instead, management has begun to take over social welfare practice, to become its technique and philosophy.

Its dominance is seen in the increasing centralization of agencies with decision-making power concentrated, as in many private companies, in an élite of managers far removed from the individuals and teams at the grass-roots. It is seen in the new language which talks of packages of care, inputs and outputs, purchasers and providers, all of which sounds more like a swarm of sales-men devoted to wringing the last penny out of customers than a social work policy which gives priority to meeting the needs of human beings. It is seen in the concept of a social service as, according to a senior consultant for accountants Price Waterhouse, 'a sharp, well-informed business'.[29] It is seen in the designation of staff respons-ible for the assessment of users' needs as 'case managers', not social workers.

This increasing power of managers within the personal social services means that often policy-making is now distant from practitioners and users. One of the strengths of the former Children's Departments was that the Chil-dren's Officers, as the directors were called, regarded themselves as social workers as well as administrators. Indeed, some carried small case-loads. Top officials thus more easily combined with the staff in direct contact with clients to agree on policy. Donnison and Chapman record how this combination successfully lobbied for the Chil-dren and Young Persons Act of 1963.[30]

Today, although directors and top managers are able and hard-working men and women, they are frequently distanced by lack of recent experience and by a long hierarchy from the front line. They do not know what it is to face an aggressive, homeless person on a Friday evening or to deal with an elderly carer who cannot cope with an even more elderly, incontinent parent. Above all, they are not close to those poverty-stricken parents caring for demanding children in a damp, overcrowded flat. Yet it is these managers who play such a large part in determining the policies and practices which affect the work lives of staff and the home lives of users.

Given the predominance of the new management, it is not surprising that it is affecting the very process of social work, which is becoming more mechanistic and less dynamic. Field workers complain that more time is spent in filling up forms, attending case reviews and arranging meetings than in relating directly with users. Within child protection the fear of making mistakes has led to 'procedural guides which are as long as short novels'.[31] Within community care, the likelihood of purchasers continually having to renegotiate contracts with providers has led one director to complain of 'the prospect of individual social workers each negotiating a totally fresh contract as a bureaucratic nightmare'.[32] Certainly, this is just what has happened in the USA where Richard Gutch reports on 'the annual paper blizzard' within 'the administrative mess of the contract state'.[33]

Moreover, these new arrangements are giving rise not just to case managers but also to a new level of management to supervise them and yet more procedures as they negotiate with the providers. No wonder that the Disability

Income Group complains that 'it threatens to add another tier of authority over the individual disabled person'.[34]

Of course, procedures have a place within any organization. The danger is that the management-devised procedures will diminish the quality of the personal relationships between practitioners and users which were once the hallmark of good social work.

Discretion and Control

It is not just that social work is becoming more mechanistic. The pressures on social workers to be cogs in a managerial chain, along with the expectation that they are a part of a business, are changing social work in two other ways—they are lessening discretion and increasing control. Traditionally, social workers have enjoyed much discretion in their relationship with users. With parents on low incomes struggling to cope with their children, for instance, social workers might have several options, such as helping them obtain a place for younger children in a nursery, assisting them to obtain the maximum preventative grant from their own department, advocating with them before the Housing Department to get better housing, giving them time-consuming support and encouragement and so on. With frail elderly persons in their own homes they will consider the input of relatives, neighbours, friends, voluntary bodies, domiciliary care, as well as their own visits.

Although supervised by senior staff, social workers have usually been trusted to make decisions about what kind of helping strategy to pursue, about how much time they devote to a particular user, and how their time is divided between various users. Probably it has been this freedom to choose how to employ their personal skills in relating with people that has given so much job satisfaction to social workers and other staff.

However, the model of social workers as workers trusted to use their own discretion does not fit easily into the New Right managerial model. In the latter, a highly centralized management determines precisely what, how and when tasks should be undertaken by lower staff, who are then checked to see that targets are being met within set budgets. This approach is now being applied to social workers who are having their tasks much more closely defined, with emphasis on not going outside a narrow brief—whatever the needs of users—and never exceeding budgets. As one assistant director, not qualified in social work himself, put it, 'Social workers who are appointed will find their advocacy role, based on social work values, being compromised by their obligations to work within a set budget'.[35] I cannot but help contrast this restrictive approach with the attitude of a former senior who accepted my judgment that a needy family needed extra resources and promised that together we would battle for them. The budget was seen as important, but so too was the effort to argue for an increased budget.

This reduction in discretion also entails a shift in skills. For instance, the emphasis on curtailing expenditure means that social workers will spend more time on administering means tests as agencies increasingly make charges for services. Accordingly, they will have less time for acting as advocates with users at DSS Reviews or in negotiating to avoid fuel cut-offs.

Significantly, Alvin Schorr, in his perceptive study of the British Social Services, links these changes in the role of social workers with lowered morale. He concluded,

'Social workers widely complain that, in a shift to administration by general managers, the purposes of their work are being subordinated and they are undervalued. This too leads to disaffection and turnover.' [36]

The New Right twins of community care legislation and budget-orientated management have thus affected the role of social workers. Within child care, the ethos of managerial control has coincided with the emergence of child abuse to influence the very purpose of social work and the personal social services. Between 1973 and 1989, 37 major inquiries were made into the deaths of children. The mass media, particularly Conservative-supporting newspapers, exploited these tragic deaths as a stick with which to attack social workers and the welfare state. Their argument was that social workers should spend less time and money on helping parents retain their children and more effort on controlling their behaviour or else removing the children. Noticeably, as Nigel Parton explains, this explanation of child neglect as just the fault of irresponsible, cruel individuals is one favoured by the New Right with its notion of a pathological underclass which must be suppressed.[37]

In fact, as Alvin Schorr concludes, it is impossible for social workers to identify potential abusers and extremely difficult to treat them.[38] None the less, political and media pressure has led many agencies to give priority to child abuse so that now, to cite Schorr, it 'tends to overwhelm children's services and the overall mission of Social Services departments'.[39] One outcome is that social workers have been pushed into closely supervising and monitoring families who might be abusers. As social work's leading academic Bill Jordan puts it, social work has 'become more coercive and restrictive', with staff checking behaviour, threatening to remove children in order to get compliance like agreeing to attend a centre for training or treatment, and sometimes denying parents access to their children when they are in care.[40]

In theory, the much vaunted Children Act of 1989 is about promoting partnership between social workers and families when children are investigated by or accommodated by local authorities. Yet, in practice, the parents may be partners with few powers or resources. Writing up a research study, Dendy Platt states, 'The child can now be removed by "agreement" but often parents have little choice—if they agree the child is taken away: if they don't they are taken to court'.[41] This paradox between the spirit of the Children Act and some social work practice was also observed by Professor Schorr. He noted that even if present at case reviews and case conferences, parents were rarely allowed to participate in any meaningful way. 'Perhaps most telling was the uniform surprise when I queried social workers about whether all parties should be consulted . . . they tend to be firm in their views that the child is their central concern and, in the end, they know what must be done. So all that went before may have been conversation, but it was not partnership.'[42]

I live close to a number of families who have faced intervention by social workers and have accompanied some to Children's Hearings. Unlike Alvin Schorr, I have worked with some social workers who take the concept of partnership seriously. But I have also met others of whom parents bitterly complain that they ignore their views and are insensitive to their feelings and circumstances. In general, partnership has not been implemented.

With control rather than partnership to the fore, it is no surprise that social work support to families in order to prevent crises is no longer a priority. The study by Gibbons and her colleagues found social workers in 'a retreat from the earlier commitment to prevention',[43] while a National Children's Bureau survey found most social workers unaware of any departmental policy on the prevention of family breakdowns.[44] This is not to say that all departments have abandoned prevention, and elsewhere I have drawn attention to the Strathclyde Preventative Initiative.[45] It is not to say that all social workers lack a belief in prevention. It is to say, as the NCB report makes clear, that supportive strategies are low in senior managers' interests and priorities and hence child care resources are devoted mainly to crisis management.

It follows that one of the main purposes of the personal social services as made plain in the Seebohm Report and of social work as put forward in the Barclay Report [46]—namely to offer support to a wide range of families in order to prevent difficulties escalating into major problems—has lost ground. Instead the resources of social work are increasingly concentrated on controlling a number of so-called high risk families. This purpose fits in exactly with the intentions of the New Right to curtail the scope of social welfare and to develop a managerial form of social work.

This does not just apply to child care. The community care legislation is making social workers into case managers who assess the needs of applicants within a context of insufficient funding. The results are already becoming clear. A survey published by *Community Care* in April 1993 to coincide with the implementation of the Community Care Act revealed three-quarters of SSDs admitting that they would be imposing stricter eligibility criteria on their services and so would expect case managers to act as rationers of resources. Indeed, research on early practice by Kathryn Ellis reveals that, in order to ration services, staff are resorting to making moral judgments about applicants by dividing them into 'the deserving and the undeserving' and even 'catching out' potential misusers of the services—and this amongst elderly and disabled people. [47] Sadly, the re-emergence of control in child care and rationing by condemnatory judgments in community care is a return to the practices of the Poor Law. Yet modern social work was supposed to replace that.

Contract Welfare

If the roles of social workers and the purposes of the personal social services are changing under New Right governments, so too is the nature of its formal relationships with the providers of care. As explained, legislation is moving local authorities into the contract culture in community care. At the same time government exhortation is encouraging it in the case of child care. Instead of relying mainly on its own facilities which are then made available to citizens, the new system entails SSDs placing contracts for services. These contracts may be placed by the authorities' purchaser sections with their own provider sections (the internal market) or with voluntary and private bodies (the external market) or with independent trusts set up by local authorities (which are somewhere between the internal and external markets). If USA trends are anything to go by—and in recent years Britain has followed American patterns—the expansion of private welfare will be the most marked. Even before the Community Care Act, 36 per cent of the budget of the SSD in Kent was going into contracts with outside firms. Immediately following the Act, Westminster City Council announced proposals to contract out £11.9 million of services, including those for elderly people, those with learning difficulties and some day care services. One month after the Act's implementation, a survey discovered that local authorities were in the process of closing or transferring to the independent sector nearly 500 of its own establishments.[48] The trend is clear. I do not deny that, for instance, some private residential homes supply good care. But overall I fear that the contract culture will lower quality for both users and staff.

Private welfare agencies are locked into the free market with its key aim of profit. This is especially true of large companies who, sniffing the prospect of material gain, entered the elderly residential scene and by 1992 owned 13.6 per cent of all private home care places. As in the privatization of gas and electricity, firms know that the easiest way to reduce costs and maximize profits is by lowering expenditure on staff. Low staff ratios are cheaper than high ones; unqualified staff cheaper than qualified ones; part-time staff with little superannuation and few holidays cheaper than full-time ones; short-term contracts cheaper than permanent ones. The signs are that such cost-cutting is occurring with adverse effects for staff and residents.

Next, private welfare will promote inconsistent care. Private residential establishments and, eventually, agencies for domiciliary care and foster care will be sold either to minimize losses or because they look a good investment to the purchaser. In 1991–92, one insolvency specialist was dealing with institutions covering 1,080 beds.[49]

Interestingly, following the implementation of the 1990

Act, owners of private residential establishments for the elderly began to complain of vacancies instead of the anticipated influx of customers. The vacancies seemed to result partly from the slowness of some SSDs in setting up their assessment systems and partly from new agencies being drawn into the market. The National Care Homes Association, representing 3,000 owners, then warned that many might now sell up because an up-turn in the property market made selling a profitable proposition. These developments well illustrate the uncertainty of the private market. And, significantly, the talk is not so much of what happens to residents but of profit and loss, with human beings being discussed as economic units. Yet these are people whose homes, lifestyles, relationships and environments are subject to upheaval and discontinuity when agencies change hands or close.

Further, to maximize profits, private welfare companies will prefer the least demanding and cheaper users. For instance, in residential care they will seek the more mobile, more healthy residents. The danger then is of a two-tier system. Private welfare will choose the least costly users and probably those able to pay something for their care. Local authorities will be left with the more frail, more poor users. Having to spend more money per person on its residential care, local authorities may then have to reduce expenditure on domiciliary care. Ironically, this outcome will undermine the stated aim of community care policy, namely to enable people to enjoy a good quality of life within their own homes.

In-house providers, plunged into the new internal market, will also find that they have to behave like private firms in cutting costs to the minimum in order to win contracts. So too will many voluntary bodies as they enter the contract culture. The large national societies probably possess the techniques and skills to formulate and win large-scale tenders. Even so, in the USA voluntary bodies have cut staff salaries by 15–20 per cent as they compete with private firms. But smaller voluntary bodies will lack the resources to compete. Significantly, a recent study of domiciliary care predicts that the wish of local authorities to give block contracts to large providers will lead to the collapse of small, local ones. Yet it is the latter whose local knowledge, flexibility and sensitivity are preferred by users.[50]

Within months of the start of the contracts system, acrimonious battles blew up. Private care home owners have taken two local authorities to court to win better deals. Others complained when SSDs awarded contracts to non profit-making trusts. Yet one SSD insisted on selling off its efficient meals service despite surveys showing that customers and staff were very satisfied. The new system centres on who gets the contracts, who gets the money, not on what is best for the users.

The former welfare system of local authorities running services themselves, supplemented by voluntary bodies and a small private market, was by no means perfect. But it did attempt to distribute services according to need rather than ability to pay, did ensure some continuity of care, did give some priority to staff training and conditions, and did back some local organizations. Under the contract culture of the New Right, these positive features are likely to be diminished.

The Acceptance of Poverty

Social welfare in general and social work in particular is subject to debate and discussion between various schools of thought. A long-running difference has been between those who favour individualistic or pathological explanations of human malfunctioning and those who see many personal problems stemming from structural causes such as the pressures of social deprivations. Within child care, Fox Harding identifies the opposing 'kinship defenders' versus 'society as parent' protagonists.[51]

These theories continue to be important within social welfare. What is not so readily acknowledged is that in addition, New Right doctrines have been making inroads into social work and welfare's beliefs and practices. Of course, I am not suggesting that social workers *en masse* have become card-carrying members of the Institute of Economic Affairs. I am saying that New Right analysis and ideology has been the most powerfully transmitted ideology in Britain in recent years and has thus created an environment in which its values become acceptable even within welfare circles.

The incorporation of New Right attitudes is most blatantly seen in the willingness of many directors and top managers of statutory Social Services to take salaries of

£50–80,000 to lead departments, some of whose users may be so poor as to suffer from malnutrition. In 1992, the aptly named Rewards Group revealed that the chief executives of national charities had received average pay increases of 30 per cent, giving them salaries of around £42,000, while their lower staff had received 6 per cent. The justification, as with the enormous local authority increases, was 'to match salaries in the private sector'.[52] In other words, social welfare incomes were to be in line with those of private enterprise firms in the competitive market. The New Right propaganda had succeeded in persuading Social Services leaders to accept basic New Right values into their personal and work lives, namely that gross inequality is acceptable alongside people like themselves taking excessive rewards and so being motivated by the greed of personal gain. More widely, numbers of personal social services staff have taken on board the concept of internal markets and the practice of the contract culture. In so doing, they have fulfilled the hopes of the free market-eers such as Friedman, Seldon and Lees and the fears of welfare state supporters such as the late Richard Titmuss.

This influence of the New Right within social welfare has three clear results. First, it has contributed to an acceptance of poverty. During the 1970s, social workers were prominent in campaigns against poverty with the British Association of Social Workers (BASW) having a well-supported Special Interest Group on poverty issues. At a practical level, social workers developed welfare rights and other skills as a means of alleviating the effects of social deprivations on individual users. The campaigning has wilted. Gibbons and her colleagues report that many social workers now feel they have 'neither the resources nor the powers to make more than a token contribution to the plight of poor families'.[53] At the top, directors can hardly protest against a poverty and inequality which is reinforced by their own large incomes.

Second, it has damaged the once noble concept of public service. There is always a temptation to exaggerate the virtues of the past. I hope I am not doing so when I recall the heyday of the local authority Children's Departments from 1948 to 1971. Then the children's officers were paid at most two to three times as much as child care officers whereas today's directors take seven or eight times as much. Perks such as high car allowances, expense accounts, trips abroad, received little attention. Few people were lured away into the trough which offered just material gain. The prevailing ethic amongst staff, administrative as well as social work, was that of serving the public.

Today standards have changed. The former chief executive of the Spastics Society left after he 'solicited business in the field of community care'.[54] Top managers will arrange to leave with golden handshakes and inflated pensions. Perhaps retiring early with a large pay-off, they then take another well-paid post. The social work magazine *Community Care* critically reports a private Home Care agency charging £3,000 to 'licence' domiciliary providers while claiming it could arrange contracts with local authorities.[55] Of course, all decline cannot be blamed on one source and there are loyal public servants who have resisted the trend. But the New Right has exalted the pursuit of private gain and sneered at state services. I believe that integrity, altruism and the concept of public servanthood become casualties in such a moral atmosphere.

Third, social workers have offered little effective resistance to New Right intrusions into the personal social services. John Findlay writes, 'Too many directors have shown astonishing enthusiasm in embracing the Government's programme of minimizing the local authority function, imposing a market culture and destroying direct provision of public services.'[56] In a study of the changes made in community care, Gary Clapton concludes, 'In a two-year search of the social work press I have been unable to find any criticisms of the proposals and legislation other than the need for more funding.'[57] It is a former director of a SSD, now Chief Inspector at the Social Services Inspectorate, who rejoices that 'The development of the mixed economy of care is steadily being achieved... the part played by the independent sector is growing in size and importance... Local authorities and their staff need to see themselves less as providers of services and more as arrangers and purchasers of services.'[58] Beverly Hughes explains that, in the face of growing poverty amongst elderly and disabled people, many personal social services staff have declined to expose and protest about the social deprivations and have concentrated on techniques for assessment, on managing budgets and public relations. She adds, 'The language of community care reflects the new managerialism which obscures inequality and deprivation.' [59]

There are exceptions. Brian Roycroft, the director of Newcastle SSD, has attacked the Government for undermining local services. But it is significant that one of the few consistent critics has been the trade union NALGO which reasons that the recent changes are shifting resources from public to private bodies, are leaving local authorities so short of money that they will be unable to help individuals on the basis of need, and are leading to a worsening of the work conditions of front-line staff.

Friedman's pleas for a dominant free market system, cuts in welfare expenditure, the reduction of statutory involvement, and the release of profit-making as the main spring of human action have all been realized. New Right doctrines, legislation and practices have had an enormous—and adverse—influence on the personal social services. Its values are rampant and rarely challenged. It is time for an alternative to be put forward.

Mutuality and Social Welfare

The New Right, to its credit, has ably communicated its values. Its academics and politicians express a belief in individual self-interest (or self and one's family) finding expression in a free market which, they claim, leads to freedom, democracy and efficiency. No doubt, not only the present establishment but also the multi-million-pound Thatcher Foundation will continue to propagate the New Right doctrines. I have tried to challenge the moral basis of its values and to question whether its policies do indeed reach the stated outcomes. The personal social services have been affected by the New Right. What can social work put in its place?

Social work has always been much concerned with values or principles. Today BASW (British Association of Social Workers) and CCETSW (Central Council in Education and Training in Social Work) take a strong and brave stand on gender and ethnic issues. Going back over thirty years to when I was a social work student, the most acclaimed text was Father Biestek's *The Casework Relationship* in which he identified the basic principles which social workers should bring into their relationships with clients. These included acceptance, confidentiality and client self-determination.[60] In 1975, BASW issued its Code of Ethics which acknowledged the 'value and dignity of every human being'. This was followed in 1980 with the helpful statement *Clients are Fellow Citizens* which puts some emphasis on clients possessing rights in their dealings with social workers, such as the right to a second opinion about their case.

Social Work Values

BASW publishes twelve principles such as 'respect for clients as individuals'; 'no prejudice in self, nor tolerance of prejudice in others, on grounds of origin, race, status, sex, sexual orientation, age, disability, beliefs, or contribution to society'; 'empowerment of clients and their participation in decisions and defining services'. These values or principles are honourable and well convey social workers' concern for their clients (or users) and their occupation. However, they have certain limitations.

First, they never explain just why all clients are to be valued, to have rights, to be regarded as citizens.

Second, outside the individual professional/client interaction, social work discussion is not strong on the nature of relationships between social workers and users. Are their interests in conflict? Are they on the same side?

Should they encourage user organizations? Should they act together with such organizations? In short, social work values tend to stress individual practice rather than collective action.

Third, in practice, as Nina Biehal explains, social work may actually disempower people.[61] Parents from whom children are removed, children being looked after by welfare agencies who are moved from placement to placement, elderly people whose complaints are not taken seriously, can be made to feel anything but valued and dignified.

Fourth, the values are not sufficiently put in a social framework. Can the dignity of individuals be promoted in an economic system which condemns some to poverty and unemployment? If not, what is the alternative which must be pursued?

Fifth, the values or principles are limited to what happens at work and do not extend to the way social workers live their lives. For instance, is it consistent for a social worker who recognizes 'the value and dignity of every human being' to live in luxury while other human beings live in cardboard boxes?

It can be seen that social work values are intensely individualistic, concentrating on the social worker's relationship with his or her client. Even when users' rights are mentioned, they are not put in a framework of how people can act together to protect rights. Of course, social work is correct to uphold the value of individuals. But a focus which minimizes consideration of mutual obligations, of environment and structures, contains certain drawbacks. For a start, it opens the door to explanations of human problems which stress the inadequacy of individuals regardless of circumstances. This individualism has something in common with that of the New Right and its conception of an underclass of feckless individuals to be condemned and controlled. Then it diminishes the resolve to campaign against poverty and other societal forces, for they are regarded as outside the real scope of social work, which is just to deal with individuals. Not least, the climate that social work is to do with a professional coping with an individual client is a barrier to social workers acting collectively with user organizations and residents of communities. Noticeably, some social work managers have been hostile to PAIN, a group of parents whose children are in public care. Again, it is rare to find professionals treating community groups in deprived areas as equals. Something more is required.

I do not claim that I have the answer. I am no longer an academic and do not possess much study time. Yet, as a neighbourhood worker on a large council estate, I do mix daily with unemployed people, recipients of Income Support, young people with no money. These are the people who suffer most from New Right policies and who, in some cases, turn to the personal social services. These experiences, in combination with my personal beliefs, lead me to call for an alternative to New Right values. I propose mutuality as a basis for social welfare.

Mutuality

Mutuality is not a common term in the discussion of values. I adapt it from the concept of fraternity which has long been a part of the radical trio of liberty, equality and fraternity. It is therefore necessary to explore the meaning of fraternity. Although less has been written about it than liberty and equality, E.J. Hobsbawm points out that it is a continuing refrain amongst workers whose jobs take them into danger, such as miners, and those who struggle for justice, such as black and other oppressed groups.[62] It becomes clear that an aspect of fraternity has been the feeling of mutual reliance or dependence within a struggle.

Amongst modern socialists, Richard Tawney has the most to say about fraternity (or, as he sometimes calls it, fellowship). In the trenches in the First World War with ordinary soldiers, Tawney found a voluntary readiness to help, even to sacrifice themselves for each other, which went beyond paid duties or orders. This fraternity he considered superior to both the arrogance of the officer class—to which he belonged by background—and to the greed of the capitalism he knew in Britain. Yet he perceived that it arose from, and was limited to, the particular conditions of danger and war. He wanted a fraternity that could be applied more generally, indeed which could be a philosophy for life. He sought its roots in God.

Tawney's starting-point is that all people are created by God. As his biographer puts it, his principles stem from a view of human beings 'neither as gods nor as cogs but as what Christianity knows as creatures'.[63] Having a common creator or parent, they are drawn together by bonds of kinship.

These ties to each other and to God contrast sharply with the New Right version that individuals should look to their own interests and particularly to their own material gain. They contrast with the dictum of T.H. Huxley, the Victorian champion of capitalism as well as evolution, who stated, 'For his successful progress man has been largely indebted to those qualities he shares with the ape and the tiger.'[64] Tawney regarded human beings as more than animals, as being capable of a motivation more than self-interest. Instead, he saw them as unique created beings who possessed spiritual attributes, that is a capacity to relate with and love God and other human creatures. He therefore looked for a society based on more than selfish materialism and sought one in which members accepted obligations to and dependence upon others simply because they were of the same kin. In his words, he looked for a fraternal society.

Tawney also drew upon Christianity to claim that not only were all people made by God but also that all had an equal standing before him. The abundance of the earth was created for all. He concluded, 'The necessary corollary, therefore, of the Christian conception of man is a strong sense of equality.'[65] Members of the human race should desire equality for their kin because this reflects both their position before God and God's intention for them. Equality implied that resources, opportunities and responsibilities should, as far as possible, be shared amongst members. Human beings who practised equality were, in Tawney's judgment, in the right or correct relationship with others. They were acting fraternally in order to promote fraternity.

The drawback to the term fraternity, derived from the word for brother, is that it has a sexist ring about it. Perhaps this is why George Lansbury strove to find other expressions. Lansbury was a working-class Christian socialist who became an MP. An early feminist, he campaigned as early as the 1880s for women to become local government representatives. In 1912 he resigned and lost his seat in the Commons over the women's issue. Years later he regained it, became a cabinet minister and eventually leader of the Labour Party. All this time, he refused to leave his East End home, declined to move from Bow Road, Poplar. His books are full of references to ordinary people whose friendship he esteemed and whose names he wished to preserve. In the preface of his *My Life*, over 60 are mentioned. He wrote of them,

'Whatever future there may be for me, my most cherished memories will be of the long, long years of work and pleasure, agitation and propaganda, carried on in company with these countless numbers of people, most of whom possess no money, no property, but who do possess the greatest of God's gifts to man, the spirt of comradeship and loyalty to each other.' [66]

Lansbury used the word comradeship where Tawney spoke of fraternity. Clearly he too means the shared values and a sense of oneness based on a common purpose. Yet the term comradeship I also find unsatisfactory as it is too closely associated with one political party. Instead I put forward the term mutuality.

Despite the differences in wording, my own position is akin to that of Tawney and Lansbury. As a Christian I give allegiance to Jesus Christ as the Son of God. This Jesus taught a responsibility towards other creatures, our neighbours. In response to the question, 'Who is my neighbour?' Jesus told the classic parable of the Good Samaritan: our obligations stretch even to those whom we do not know, to all those who are in need. Christ's radical teachings resulted in his death upon the cross. For Christians like me, the cross is the way to forgiveness, to atonement. Yet, as the Archbishop of Canterbury, George Carey, puts it, 'We must reject as unbiblical any attempt to privatize the atonement, as if the only salvation that Christ had in mind was spiritual and other worldly.'[67] The cross, Carey continues, also embodies the practice that we must be prepared to make sacrifices for others as an expression of our love for and ties to them.

It is this 'neighbour principle' put into action which I call mutuality. It was carried out by the early church where members shared possessions with each other. It was upheld by the apostle Paul who urged, 'And look out for one another's interest, not just for your own.' Further, when writing to a group of believers, he advised generosity to others, saying, 'At the moment your surplus meets their needs, but one day your need may be met from their surplus. The aim is equality.'[68]

I then take mutuality to encompass the principles and values so well expressed by Tawney and so well practised by Lansbury. The dictionary defines mutuality as a feeling or action which conveys affection and benefit towards each other. This discussion leads me to make a fuller explanation. Mutuality is:

the recognition of mutual obligations towards others,

stemming from the acceptance of a common kinship,

expressed in joint action,

towards a more equitable sharing of resources and responsibilities.

It thus contains an assumption about the nature of our ties to other people, an objective which is to press towards greater equality, and a form of action which is co-operative.

I regard mutuality as the principle which should guide our behaviour towards others. It is a principle which can both set our objectives and shape our daily conduct. It is a principle which can influence both our relationships with individuals and the structures we try to develop in society's institutions. Personally, I have sometimes, certainly not always, enjoyed mutuality within churches. I have experienced it within a small and struggling branch of the Labour Party on a council estate. Perhaps most of all I found it with the helpers, users and staff at the Southdown Community Project in Bath. Here I had daily contact with a group of people who shared similar values and objectives, who did not want perks or over-time pay, who were protective of each other, who cared about the interests of others, in whose cause they were prepared to make personal sacrifices. During the last seven years in the large Easterhouse estate I have wit-nessed mutuality as residents, many of them surviving on Income Support, have banded together for the common good.

Clearly, I am drawing heavily on Christianity for my concept of mutuality and I regard it as one aspect of the working out of God's kingdom on earth. Members of other faiths may object that my deductions are too Christian. However, my understanding of some other major reli-gions, limited though it is, is that they too conceive of a God who is both creator and love. It follows that they too can make similar deductions about mutuality. Some may object to any reference to a God. Interestingly, there are contemporary writers, such as Ruth Lister, who draw on the fact that we are all citizens as the unifying bond.[69] The proponents of mutuality may disagree on the source which binds them together, but agree that human beings possess similar features which require them to treat each other in ways which uphold, not demean, their common humanity.

The concept of mutuality, or its like, is not in vogue. To the hard-headed, profit-obsessed New Right it appears as sentimental softness. To a newer breed of Labour Party members, concerned with expediency and image, it may appear as tea and buns in the co-op hall. These dismissals stem from misunderstandings about mutuality, so it is necessary to clarify four points.

First, mutuality is not unpractical. It may sound and indeed is idealistic. Yet it also implies a straightforward application. If other human beings are our kin, they can be called our mutuals, then we can make judgments about their social conditions by reference to our own. For instance, in Britain I would not wish to survive on £7,000 a year with my children having a high vulnerability to bronchitis, accidents, low educational attainment, even early death. It follows that I cannot tolerate it for other families.

Second, mutuality is more than a feeling of affection, more than a warm glow in the company we enjoy. I recall an affluent friend illustrating her radicalism by saying how well she got on with her low-paid cleaning lady. Well-meaning as the remark is, it is made possible by an enforced social gap between two human beings. Mutuality may well entail affection and 'getting on' but it is also based on a recognition that our kin should not be separated from us by huge differences in status, power and income. Mutuality must be based upon right relationships.

Third, mutuality is not anti-individual. Friedman makes much of his claim that collective state action leads to the repression of individuals. So it has in the totalitarian states where he made his analysis. But such repression also occurs in fascist states which embrace capitalism and the market. By contrast, mutuality values every individual because all individuals have common roots, common needs and common rights to all that is best in society. If anything, mutuality enlarges individualism because members have to accept responsibilities for others as well as themselves.

But, fourth, mutuality goes beyond individualism because it is also about creating different structures which enable mutuality to flourish. The best soil for mutuality is one in which self-interest, inequality and competition are matched by the alternatives of greater altruism, equality and co-operation. Obviously, the attainment of such profound changes will require political action just as did those brought about by the New Right. Of course, there are limits. R.H.Tawney was clear that democratic reform was necessary as the foundation for what he called fraternity. But he added that new social conditions could only facilitate fraternity, not impose it. The same applies to mutuality. Terrill explains that if the barriers of class, power and wealth are removed then 'The citizens would simply be within reach of each other.'[70] Such radical redistribution of resources would not impose mutuality. They would make it more possible, they would make it more open to choice.

Mutuality offers an alternative value base to that of the New Right. The latter encourages citizens to be concerned for themselves and their immediate family. Mutualists, while accepting family bonds, also base their actions on a sense of obligation to, and responsibility for, the well-being of others. The New Right asserts that humankind's integral self-interest should be allowed full vent in a competitive, free-market system almost untouched by statutory limitations. Mutualists conceive of human nature as both selfish and unselfish and look to an economic system which promotes the latter. Mutuality is thus a principle or value which can be applied to the whole of life. Here, however, I am mainly concerned with its application to social welfare. I shall focus on the personal social services and their staff, particularly social workers.

4

Public Provision

The initial question is, who should own or run the personal social services? The concept of mutuality, of fraternity, entails a commitment to the best welfare for all our kin, that is for all people. It entails the promotion of a co-operative environment in which people are regarded as unique and valuable humans, not as economic units. It entails the building of mechanisms to spread resources more equally so that access to the best care is not dependent on personal wealth or power but upon personal need.

I do not see how these ends can be attained with a culture and system dominated by market mechanisms in which the ruling motive is private profit and whose management is geared to the winning or granting of tenders. Instead I advocate a welfare system in which services are provided directly by local authorities, supplemented by voluntary bodies and community groups. I would not call for the prohibition of private welfare, for a free society must allow that option. However, the bulk of public funding should be employed mainly to run high quality services or to grant-aid non-profit making groups to do the same. The funds themselves should come not from charges imposed upon users but from government taxation drawn according to people's incomes. In short, the public system is a mechanism for the redistribution of resources.

The New Right bases much of its case for the privatization of welfare on three factors: increased efficiency, choice and democracy. In fact, it is public welfare which promotes these virtues, along with the added bonus of stability.

Efficiency

Efficiency and inefficiency may occur within both statutory and private welfare. None the less, the straightforward public provision of services possesses definite advantages. As explained, the market process, whether internal or external, introduces more staff and extra layers of bureaucracy. An early study of contracts for attendance schemes for disabled people concludes that it ties up staff in complex negotiations and hence promotes lengthy delays.[71]

Further, if efficiency means reaching those in greatest need, then direct public provision has the edge over the market. A study by Age Concern in London revealed that the new approach of cutting local authority provision and bringing in contract care had resulted in the former having to cut its home help services, so leaving a gap which the market failed to fill because it was not financially attractive.

The consequence was the neglect of some needy people.[72] Not least, the market approach has little time for preventative savings. Profit-orientated agencies concentrate on immediate provision such as residential care, where demand is obvious and there is a quick return. They are less interested in preventative approaches which result in longer-term savings for the community. Yet, clearly, investment in domiciliary services can avoid future expensive institutional care for the elderly.

In child care, as early as 1952 a Select Committee in the House of Commons was pointing out the economic savings resulting from policies to keep children in their own homes.[73] Thus, by avoiding the complexities of contract negotiations, by using resources according to need, and by backing prevention, local authorities can be more efficient than the private sector.

Choice

The New Right claims that choice is synonymous with private welfare. Its argument is that a market offers a variety of goods where people buy what suits their needs. The community care legislation is designed to encourage private welfare in general and, in particular, to direct elderly and disabled people to case managers who will assess their needs and then decide which service to buy them with agencies with which contracts have been placed. These contracts are increasingly with the independent sector, that is private and voluntary bodies and, indeed, the

Government has decreed that 85 per cent of money transferred to local authorities for community care must be
spent here. They will be decreasingly with local government agencies who are strapped for cash. In 1993 it was
estimated that local authorities were short of £135 million
needed to implement community care.[74]

Far from increasing choice, the new system will have the
opposite effect. First, it should be recalled that the private
market offers real choice only to buyers who can afford it.
Low-income citizens, whatever their need, cannot purchase high-cost residential care or 24-hour home nursing
any more than they can afford private boarding-school fees
for their children. Even when assisted by state subsidies to
purchase residential care for the elderly, the choice is more
apparent than real. It is not like buying tea-bags, where
various brands are on offer along with the alternative of
coffee. Consumers in the private welfare market tend to
lack information about the range of services available to
them. They might follow up an advertisement for a local
Home but its owners will not give details of other Homes
and will not encourage domiciliary care if their basic
concern is to fill a bed. Individual consumers have little
real choice unless very well equipped with money and
information.

It can be argued that, under the new community system,
low-income citizens will have case managers to advise them
and, after a means test, to ensure some financial backing.
However, second, the case manager/contracts system has
inbuilt drawbacks. The new contracts are expected to be

increasingly with profit-making companies. They tend to favour residential care and hence potential users will have limited access to private domiciliary care. The case managers are thus likely to find themselves in the same position as those in the USA where an evaluation found them directing people into what the market wanted, not what the applicants requested. The case managers were conveyers of persuasion, not choice.[75]

Third, as local authority resources are being cut, it follows that SSDs will be less able to offer council residential care to those who prefer it to private care, or domiciliary help for those choosing to remain at home. The lack of choice is sharply illustrated in a Government statement that local authorities cannot spend more than £500 a week on domiciliary services to enable severely disabled people to stay in their own homes. Unless possessed of considerable private means they 'will be expected to go into residential care or nursing homes'.[76] Some choice. Already research into the community care practices of four SSDs is giving warning signs. It found that the care managers often could not offer choice because the market was not attracting sufficient providers. Yet social workers were so taken up with managerial tasks that they could not pursue developmental functions to stimulate more provision. Users were given little information about the system and those with private money still fared best. Pessimism was common amongst staff and users.[77] This is the present road for community care and is one which child care is just joining. Far more straightforward would be a properly funded system of public provision offering a variety of residential establishments and extensive domiciliary help together with information about both. Such a system is more likely to promote more choice for more people.

Democracy

The New Right has also defended the new community care legislation on the grounds that its market approach is more democratic, in that it hands power to users. Oddly enough, recent market research reveals user groups complaining that the new market-led management has little time for them.[78] Belatedly, the Government has appointed the National Users and Carers Group to advise on community care implementation. Users have just two places out of 21 members. But they are not elected, not even chosen by bodies of users. As in all quangos, they are the appointees of central government ministers. Quangos, privately-run agencies, even independent trusts, all have the same defect. They are not directly responsible to the electorate. Services provided by local authorities outside market forces are likely to be more democratic.

Of course, resources are finite and statutory bodies will always have to make decisions about who can be helped and how. But, under the direct public provision approach, decisions are not biased according to what powerful private agencies decide to offer and what people can pay. The users' voice counts for more. Further, in the end, local authorities are answerable to the electorate. True, democracy has its limitations and citizens can feel distanced from officials and councillors. Yet I live on an estate where a threatened school closure was averted by parents and other residents voicing their views to elected representatives. There are examples of inmates of local authority homes uniting to lobby their councillors about their complaints. This is more democratic than one in which redress can only be sought by approaches to directors or shareholders whose primary loyalty is to profitability. But social service democracy will only flourish if staff and users are committed to it and if it is free from the grip of the market system. It requires the values of mutuality rather than those of the New Right.

The advantages of direct public provision are highlighted by looking at its opposite, the contractual, internal marketing and extensive private welfare across the Atlantic. Professor Alvin Schorr, himself an American, explains that independent agencies in the child care field want contracts which deal with a set number of children—such as treating child abusers or finding foster homes—not ones which deal with extensive neighbourhoods. The result has been the decline of preventative services and the decline of neighbourhood participation in services. In regard to community care, the system has been swamped by bureaucracy in which individual choice drowns.[79]

Anyone who has been to the USA will know that poor people have little welfare choice and less democracy. Public-led services can modify these disadvantages just as they can avoid the fluctuations of the market system in which private welfare agencies are sold or closed in order to suit private pockets.

So public provision can be within a context of efficiency, choice, democracy and stability. Those who hold the values of mutuality insist on these ends, because they hold that they are the due of all, no matter how weak their economic position.

5

The Supportive Services

Given that the personal social services should be largely in the hands of public bodies, what objectives or priorities should they set? Most of us do not want to have our children removed and taken into care, we do not want our family functioning damaged by extreme environmental stress, in old age we do not want to be placed in institutions against our will. Mutuality means that the disadvantages we wish to avoid for ourselves will not be placed upon others.

The deduction is that the main purpose of the personal social services should be to support families (and individuals) vulnerable to these disadvantages. It should be to prevent them reaching the point where intervention and control is placed upon them. Within the blight of the enormous contemporary social deprivations, the aim should be to modify the devastating effects of social inequalities which now ruin the lives of so many. The purpose applies to the elderly, the disabled, the chronically sick, indeed to all the user categories for which the personal social services have responsibility. Here, however, I shall illustrate it mainly by reference to families whose care of their children bring them to the notice of the authorities.

Of course, statutory agencies must have a duty to protect children even if it requires removing them from their homes. As a former social worker, I occasionally exercised that duty. Yet in recent years child protection has dominated child care work with corresponding less attention to support and prevention. It is encouraging that, since the implementation of the Children Act (1989), the number of emergency protection orders has dropped compared with previous place of safety orders which they replaced. But this may be because they are harder to obtain rather than because families are better supported.

Ironically, the Children Act which seeks a better balance between the rights of children and responsibilities of parents has been followed by government restrictions which have led some SSDs to have to curtail services. Some London boroughs have 25 per cent of child care cases unallocated to social workers. Other departments are shedding staff so that the main priority of the remaining members becomes immediate intervention to deal with crises rather than prior action to diminish the rise of emergencies. I will discuss the issue of resources later. Here I suggest that positive prevention or enabling support requires a facility approach allied with community social work.

A Facility Approach

Living in Easterhouse, I see how difficult it is for some families to obtain facilities which others take for granted—a dry flat, a new cooker, a holiday, a removal van, cheap credit. It may even be hard to afford a decent funeral. I accompanied a young woman who was reduced to tears by the cheapest estimate to bury her father, £1,100. The impossibility of getting such essential items and services can ultimately overwhelm some people.

There can even be barriers to obtaining services which local authorities have the powers to provide. Consider day care for young children. In reviewing the research, Cannan explains that well-run nurseries, day care centres, play groups etc. can benefit both children and parents. The former gain from social interaction with other children. The latter may be freed to seek employment or just enjoy a break from child care.[80] Yet families who cannot afford to buy or to travel to such care may be offered it by local authorities only if they are regarded as potential or actual abusers. This condition may inhibit some from applying while stigmatizing those who do. My argument is that local authorities should offer supportive facilities, such as day care, after-school clubs, play schemes, to neighbourhoods with access depending upon residence rather than being assessed as a problem.

The evidence suggests that most families cope with themselves and their children if sufficient resources are available to them. These facilities should be supplemented by family aides, homemakers and social workers for those wanting more intensive and personal help. Similarly, in regard to community care, residential homes and day centres would be facilities open to communities and supplemented by home helps, meals on wheels, transport, and other forms of domiciliary care.

The facility approach would necessitate some shift in the strategy of the personal social services, with the provision of straightforward neighbourhood services being considered as worthy as counselling and treatment to individuals. In this respect, it is worth recording two of the findings of Gibbons and her colleagues' study, that parents 'showed more improvement in parenting problems if they made any use of day care' and that users particularly appreciated those social workers able to link them with community facilities.[81]

Community Social Work

These facilities should be maintained within a context of community social work. In 1982, the Barclay Report defined community social work as social work which 'seeks to tap into, support, enable, and underpin the local networks of formal and informal relationships'.[82] It was recommended as a means of preventing personal crises through strengthening local communities.

In response, at least a quarter of local authorities did decentralize their personal social services teams into neighbourhood patches. Here social workers and other staff used the approaches of entering into community life, recruiting local help and offering immediate practical support. But the community social work summer was brief. The continuing media and political pressure for concentration on immediate interventions into child abuse cases won the battle for resources. An increasingly macho management, influenced by business models, had little sympathy for the delegation of powers to local teams and many were soon drawn back into centralized and hierarchical systems.

Yet community social work never died and recent studies are reaffirming its value. On the Canklow Estate, the Rotherham SSD initiated a small team based on a community centre which was accessible to residents, welcomed callers with practical difficulties, linked them with local amenities, and acted with residents to form play schemes, women's groups, youth clubs and education classes. The results, published by its leader Derek Eastham, reveal that numbers of children in care and on supervision declined markedly. Most significant was the drop to almost zero of those on the 'at risk' register. No longer feeling stigmatized and threatened, families came at an early stage of their difficulties. The locally-run groups boosted members' confidence as well as relieving some environmental stress.[83]

In Oldham, Steve Rogowski reported that community social work led to an increase in informal callers but a dramatic 85 per cent drop in official referrals.[84] These and other studies reflect earlier ones which shaped the Barclay recommendations. They do not claim that community social work can cope with every type of case, but they do confirm that it is both applicable to statutory cases and also preventative in outcome.

It should be added that community social work is not limited to child care and family work. The action research of Bayley and his colleagues found it to be just as valuable for elderly and disabled clients. Its proximity and informality encouraged them to call at offices where they could obtain full information about the available residential and domiciliary services. The links with neighbourhood activities—together with on-the-spot provision of practical aids—meant that human and material support was soon in their own homes. Not least, as at Canklow, the community social workers were able to offer their premises to residents to use for their groups.[85]

Community social work should be the core of the personal Social Services. It has much in common with mutuality. It minimizes the distance between expert professionals and users. It maximizes local involvement and affirms the importance of neighbours and community activities. It emphasizes that ordinary people have obligations for each other. Community social work is preventative and thus in accord with the duties laid upon local authorities by the Children Act (1989) to enable children, if possible, to stay with their own families. It can prevent some families reaching the point where their quality of life, even their liberty, is destroyed.

The application of mutuality, then, leads initially to an emphasis on public services which are responsive to needs rather than to a market, which facilitate users' coping mechanisms, which are rooted in neighbourhoods, and which are preventative. They are thus in contrast with those developments ushered in during the era of the New Right which have encouraged the independent, profit-led sector; which have favoured managerial power rather than neighbourhood participation, and which have opted for protection rather than prevention in child care. At least, the fact that, in the long run, prevention does save money should appeal also to the New Right.

Family Centres

Family centres have been a peripheral if important part of the personal social services. Yet the track record of some centres and their affinity with mutuality suggests they should play a more central role.

The Children Act (1989) describes family centres as places where family members may attend for occupational, social, cultural or recreational activities and for advice, guidance or counselling. A survey by Warren in 1989 enumerated 352 family centres in England and Wales of which 57 per cent were run by statutory bodies and 43 per cent by voluntary agencies.[86]

Two main kinds of centres have been identified. The client-focused model concentrates mainly on clients referred for child abuse or neglect and provides skilled and intensive treatment for a small number of children and, usually, mothers. The neighbourhood model is open to the local community and offers activities such as day care, play schemes, women's groups, after-school clubs, welfare rights advice.

In recent years, the former model has gained favour, with Warren estimating that 70 per cent of centres concentrate on child protection functions. Cannan attributes this shift to 'a more authoritarian stance in child care work ... whose directors of Social Services ... emphasized monitoring and treatment rather than prevention and community social work'.[87] To be sure, such centres do enable a small number of women to learn or accept child management skills in a protected environment. But sometimes they feel they are forced to attend on threat of losing their children.

The centres are also criticized on the grounds that they imply that child care is the responsibility of mothers, not fathers. Further, the centres are often closed to local residents and, being restricted, tend to impose a stigma on those who do attend. Stigma is a feeling of social disgrace, shame or inadequacy which can lower self-esteem, reduce confidence, provoke isolation and so actually reinforce personal difficulties.

While not excluding a role for client-focussed centres, the advantages of the neighbourhood approach are more numerous. Studies give the following findings.

First, neighbourhood family centres are popular. Their openness, informality and accessibility—usually in the middle of neighbourhoods—means that no barriers are erected. Moreover, as Gibbons and her research colleagues recorded, they reach 'families with the greatest need'.[88] The same study admits that the presence of such families does sometimes put off some more coping families. But generally a wide range of users are drawn in, including some with alleged child abuse difficulties, to an environment which conveys no stigma, simply because it does not concentrate on one type of problem.

Second, the diverse number of activities means that a variety of staff work together. Gibbons and her team found that the centres they studied 'were rarely led by professional social workers'.[89] Some were qualified social workers, others held youth and community work, nursery nursing, play group, teaching or no qualifications. Consequently, the centres were identified with the facility approach, not the interventionist style often associated with modern social work.

Third, the centres were marked by much local participation. Residents certainly came to use the facilities. In addition, some then became involved as helpers, volunteers, part-time staff and, in some cases, as full-time staff. As I discovered in a study of family centres, residents who became staff, even project leaders, often enriched the work by their unique understanding of local needs and dynamics.[90]

Fourth, users do benefit. Studies are in agreement that users tend to find their isolation reduced, their self-confidence raised, their skills extended. In short, the quality of their lives is, if only moderately, improved. Cannan, in her investigation, explains that 'it is current stresses in families which may tip the balance between coping and not coping'.[91] Neighbourhood centres with their supportive, non-condemnatory approaches can tip it towards coping and so prevent family breakdowns and disintegration.

The participatory emphasis of family centres encourages the acceptance of common obligations which is the essence of mutuality. By no means do they attract all residents in happy teamwork. Cliques and local mafia may try to dominate some centres and so put off other residents. But, as I pointed out in a study of family centres, they generally do succeed in drawing together a variety of people who then act jointly towards agreed objectives. This closeness strengthens members as individuals and also enables them to strengthen others.[92] Simultaneously, the mixing together of different kinds of staff and their constant interaction with residents serves to break down barriers between staff and users. The former cannot look upon the latter just as recipients or clients. The walls of class, status and professional elitism are thus pulled down in a building-yard of greater equality.

To date, family centres have concentrated mainly on families with dependent children. But this need not invariably be so. The one with which I was associated in Southdown also drew in elderly persons for their own activities, as volunteers and as committee members. Elderly people are members of families, and the future developments of family centres must include making a place for their needs and contributions.

Family centres draw in a wide variety of users but they do not exclude individuals with severe personal problems. On the contrary, my experience is that they can more easily walk into a centre which is not marked out as a place for those with particular difficulties. In addition, the wide-ranging community outlook enables residents to regard the personal social services in a far more positive light than is often the case. For all this to happen, however, family centres must be far more numerous than at present. The concept of mutuality thus leads to a picture of a new organizational structure for the personal social services, one in which a facility approach, community social work and family centres are the foundation.

6

Meeting the Needs of the Community

Social work concern for poverty has declined. Yet poverty should be a major issue for the personal social services. Poverty is extensive, with the young and elderly particularly at risk. In 1989, 3,780,000 children, 30 per cent of the child population, were dependent upon incomes at about Income Support levels. In 1987, elderly people made up 31 per cent of all those classified as poor. Not surprisingly, Gibbons and her researchers identified material problems as now the most common reason why people approach the SSDs.[93] They may come simply because they are desperate for a cooker, a fire, a bed, even food. They may come because the conditions and pressures of poverty contribute to their personal problems. Noticeably, the majority of children now looked after by local authorities are the children of the poor.

The existence of poverty is inconsistent with mutuality, a mutuality which involves a concern for other people as our kin. I have been close to a family whose father, despairing after years of unemployment, killed himself. The mother has struggled bravely for years on Income Support. Once she asked me to persuade one of her sons to tidy his bedroom. It contained no wardrobe, no cupboards—no wonder it was untidy. There was no radiator to dry the damp patches. Just beds. About that time I read that the Government minister Michael Heseltine lived in a £3 million estate replete with pheasants and trout lakes. As a mutualist, I cannot accept that some of my kin lack necessities while others enjoy needless luxuries. A society, and within it a system of personal social services, built on the concept of mutuality, must seek both to alleviate poverty and to reduce differences.

The Attack on Poverty

The attack on poverty will require a strategy, skills, practice and pressure. The personal social services will need a strategy that deploys resources to be of maximum use to poor people. Clearly this will involve both locating extra resources in areas of social deprivation and also delivering them in ways which do not humiliate or demean the recipients. As indicated, community social work and family centres appear to be the mechanisms for achieving these ends. The staff in these agencies will need to be adept at the skills which convey welfare rights advice, which negotiate with creditors, which accompany users to DSS reviews, which link them with grant-giving bodies.

These skills should be as much a part of training courses as those concerning child abuse.

If less poverty and greater equality are to be objectives of the personal social services then their members should practise them within their own agencies. At present, welfare agencies pay both the highest and lowest of salaries, with the gap between a director of Social Services and a care assistant as great as that between a private capitalist and a cleaner. Members of the personal social services, both elected representatives and officials, if truly motivated by mutuality, should strive for internal wage structures which reduce differences and so enter into what Tawney called the proper relationship with our kin. This will involve self-denial for some, but the greater equality implied in the concept of mutuality cannot be attained unless principles are put into practice.

Social work skills can alleviate, not abolish poverty. Thus obtaining people's full welfare rights benefits usually improves their income but without lifting them out of poverty. The overriding need is for national policies to abolish social deprivations. Social workers, through their trade unions and professional bodies, and in alliance with users, should be more prominent in the campaign against poverty. Social workers and other staff in the personal social services are often close to the most poverty-stricken people in our society. Their knowledge, if publicized, might at least keep poverty on the national agenda.

I live and work in an area where two-thirds of school children receive clothing grants, that is they come from families with very low incomes. Many parents are unemployed, many families dwell in damp tenements, some elderly people cut down on heat and food just to survive. It is easy to feel overwhelmed and say 'What's the use? What can we do in the midst of these structural deprivations?'

The positive fact is that the input of social service staff can have some effect. The Gibbon study of social workers certainly detected some defeatism in the face of poverty. But it also found that, where social workers did tackle the practical difficulties of families, it contributed to a 'significant positive association with improvement in parenting problems.'[94]

In Strathclyde, an initiative by the SWD which helped poor parents, whose children were seriously at risk of reception into care, by giving them substantial rather than paltry financial grants recorded, after a follow-up, that 91 per cent of the children were still with their parents. The cash had led to a raising of material standards and the relief of tension which then allowed parents to develop their caring capacities.[95] In the 1980s, Strathclyde also conducted a welfare rights campaign to ensure that people received their full entitlements. It led to them receiving £1.3 million extra a year in weekly payments and £2.75 million in single payment grants.

Poverty can be alleviated, individual families can be helped by the personal social services. Nor should campaigning for more fundamental reforms be discounted just because progress appears slow. People such as George

Lansbury and Will Crooks lived in even more unpromising times at the peak of the capitalist sweat-shops and the horror of the workhouse. Yet they possessed a faith which convinced them that such practices were evil and a courage to organize against them. Eventually they won some modification of the former and the abolition of the latter. They were motivated and strengthened by 'love, co-operation and brotherhood',[96] that is by the spirit of mutuality.

The Collective Community

In advocating public services, I do not mean to imply statutory monopoly. In most socially-deprived areas, particularly in the inner cities and the sprawling, peripheral housing estates, can be found the often overlooked community groups. Unlike the national voluntary societies they are local in nature and weak in resources. They possess no royal patrons or prestigious committees. Made up mainly of local residents, they run tenants' associations, furniture stores, food co-ops, play schemes, welfare rights projects, day-care centres, credit unions, community transport schemes and so on. This is the collective community whose activities have much in common with mutuality.

Their thriving existence kicks away another prop of the underclass theory. In Easterhouse, which Murray cites as one of the classic examples of the underclass community,[97] there are over 300 such groups. The unemployed and lone parents, whom Murray describes as feckless and irresponsible, play their part within these organizations.

Their devotion and reliability demonstrates the positive characteristics of many citizens who are branded an underclass. They still remain poor and unemployed, but clearly the responsibility cannot be laid at the door of their fecklessness.

The community groups have a further significance in that they thrive on user involvement. There is not the great social and physical distance between decision-makers and users found in large, bureaucratic machines. The controllers of community groups are usually elected annually by local residents. Often they are unemployed, on Income Support, and know what it is to be a client of the personal social services. It follows that they are knowledgeable about local needs, are in touch with local demands, and answerable to local users of their agency. The chairperson of the Food Co-op will have a dissatisfied customer knock on the door. As an employee of a project which runs youth and family activities, I will be stopped in the street by committee members or parents to be told their opinions of what I am doing. This combination of participation and democracy is unusual. Certainly it stands in contrast to present trends by which the Government is increasing the centralized power of Whitehall and reducing local democracy by setting up appointed quangos, mainly of business people, to oversee health boards, police committees and urban development corporations.

The collective community also stands as an alternative to profit-motivated enterprises. Food co-ops offer a range of cheap goods. They might have a turnover of £100,000 a year, but this is not converted into profits for shareholders or exorbitant salaries. Consequently, food is cheap. The small co-op in our neighbourhood sells bread at 27p a loaf as against 50p on the local vans. Credit unions provide loans at 12.6 per cent APR which is half the rate of private companies and a fraction of that charged by loan sharks. Day-care schemes offer reliable care at reasonable prices.

These practical enterprises prove that personal greed and self-interest do not have to be the motivation for the supply of goods and services. They demonstrate that provision does not have to fit into the business model of contracts. They show that individuals are prepared to work hard for the benefit of others, that the bond between supplier and user can be one of co-operation. Contrary to Adam Smith's assertion, supply does not have to depend upon the material self-interest of the supplier.

They can also stand for a clearer definition of the word 'profit'. If they are going to carry on trading next year as well as this, the 'businesses' such as co-ops will need to make a proper surplus, or profit, for investing in new stock. Otherwise they will quickly run out of cash and go out of business. Like any other small business, it is essential that they set out their likely income and expenditure to ensure that they are charging enough for their goods and services to ensure that they do not run out of cash. But this form of 'capitalism' is a slave, not a master. Profit here does not imply higher salaries or returns for investors. The motivation is not that of profit but of helping the community—and this is crucial if the ventures are to succeed.

The collective community is essentially mutual. Its groups contain members who accept obligations towards others not from a desire to inflate their own wallets and pensions but from a recognition that they are tied together by common bonds. This recognition is worked out in co-operative action with members uniting closely together.

The spirit of mutuality must not be overstated. Having worked in the community for over 17 years, I know that participants can argue, blow up, walk out. I also know that more frequently they display a readiness to sacrifice themselves, a commitment towards others and an enjoyment of others' company which justifies the description of mutuality.

Not least, the collective community has leanings towards greater equality. The services of the groups are usually for the benefit of citizens who are in the bottom 10 per cent of society's income recipients. Further, they operate with little regard for status, with no undue bowing to qualifications, with no desire for members to earn themselves MBEs or other establishment gongs. Salaries, where given, are never high because it is accepted that resources must be shared for the good of all. Indeed, some groups ensure that all salaries, be they for project leaders or cleaners, are paid on the same basis.

Community groups thus promote mutuality while doing nothing to promote inequality. Anyone wanting personal social services based on the values of mutuality will want a place for the collective community. Yet there is another reason. Like family centres, community groups are a source of strength to those families most vulnerable to social disadvantages. They can support them and do so in ways which convey no stigma and which are acceptable to all. Food co-ops can ensure a more adequate and extensive diet for poor families. Credit unions can provide a low interest loan for, say, a new cooker, so allowing parents to avoid the indignity of applying for a Social Fund loan or the danger of being sucked dry by a loan shark. Play schemes and after-school clubs can mean stimulus for children and relief for hard-pressed parents. In addition, the very involvement of the same families in the running of or membership of the groups can reduce their isolation and extend their capacities. Significantly, the conclusion of Gibbons and her colleagues, after studying the preventative work of SSDs and community projects, was to confirm the hypothesis that 'parents under stress more easily overcome family problems... when there are many sources of family support available in local communities'.[98]

Community groups depend much upon grants from local authorities. Unfortunately, they tend to be the Cinderellas, receiving less recognition and money than the more traditional voluntary societies. Ironically, too, just as the recession has escalated distress within socially-deprived neighbourhoods, so local authorities are having to cut their grants still more. By contrast, my argument is that from now on local authorities should incorporate community groups fully into their social strategies, treating them not as supplicants to be satisfied with a few coppers but as essential services to be regarded as and financed as seriously as main-line provision.

7

Which Way Forward?

It may be helpful if I first summarize the positions I have described.

The New Right has been the dominant force in Britain during the last 15 years. In regard to social welfare, its policy-makers advocate curtailing the powers and costs of local authorities and shifting provision into the competitive market. Its blueprint for the personal social services, partly achieved, partly in the making, has the following characteristics:

1. Less direct provision of services by local authorities. These include services which come under the community care umbrella, such as residential homes for the elderly, day care for people with special needs and domiciliary services, as well as services for children and families such as children's homes, foster care, the supervision of child protection.

2. Increased provision by the so-called independent sector made up of private profit-making firms and

traditional voluntary societies.

3.   Services to be provided through private firms, voluntary bodies and the local authorities' own agencies tendering for contracts, to be placed by the local authorities' purchasing arm.

4.   The role of many social workers changing to case managers, who assess the needs of applicants and then devise 'packages' of services to be placed with those bodies which have won contracts.

5.   The centrality of a business approach which believes that the market economy is the best means of cutting costs and achieving efficiency.

6.   In regard to families and child care, the giving of low priority to support and prevention and high priority to controlling and treating alleged abusing families. The alleviation of poverty to be considered peripheral to the work of the personal social services.

7.   In general, a shift towards a form of social work which is managerial, in which market forces rather than public services are esteemed, and in which individual private and material gain rather than collective concern and action is considered sufficient motive for staff.

In response, and taking mutuality as the foundation stone, I have proposed personal social services marked by the following:

1. Properly-funded public services directly run by elected local authorities supplemented by the independent sector.

2. The role of social welfare staff, in direct contact with users, to be that of identifying with them and advocating on their behalf, in order to get the best services appropriate to their needs. They should be orientated towards equipping families and individuals with the resources that enable them to cope with their own lives and prevent personal difficulties escalating into major problems.

3. Services which are offered as facilities to neighbourhoods and not restricted to stigmatized individuals.

4. Community social work teams and family centres— whether housed together or in separate premises—as the main locations of social welfare activity.

5. The development of agency strategies and staff skills to alleviate the impact of social deprivations along with the acceptance of a responsibility to campaign against poverty.

6. SSDs and SWDs giving some priority to strengthening and extending local community groups.

7. A prevailing ethic in which not only is there a commitment towards the promotion of the kind of services we would desire for our kin but also the involvement of our kin in their promotion: mutuality.

Objections

The concept of mutuality will meet criticisms and objections. In lecturing and talking about it I am encouraged by the response, but three objections are mooted. One is that in the past groups which have been bound together by ties of affection and common interest have often been hostile to, have even rejected, outsiders. Anne Phillips cites the example of craft unions which looked after their own but tried to keep apart from others.[99] Tawney recognized this limitation when he enjoyed the comradeship of ordinary soldiers in the trenches. The same soldiers despised their officers and hated the Germans. Tawney thereafter constructed his fraternity based not on class, occupation, rank or nationality but on a common creation.

The same goes for mutuality. It casts its net wide. It is an attempt to promote mutual obligations amongst all human beings. Nonetheless, mutualists will provoke conflict, for instance, those who on the basis of mutuality call for the kinds of changes in the personal social services as outlined in this book will meet the hostility of those who have enriched themselves from the welfare industry and those who want welfare embedded in the market economy.

Yet attitudes of mutuality must still be extended towards opponents, for they too are our kin. The implications concern the methods which mutualists will use to advance their cause. They will organize, publicize, argue, campaign. They will not smear, lie, shout down, hate, for so to do contradicts the respect they must hold for all their kin. Perhaps the supreme injunction is that of Jesus Christ to 'love your enemies'. The supreme example comes in his life and death. To repeat, I am not equating mutuality with the Christianity to which I give allegiance. I am claiming that its founder expressed a respect for others, a graciousness, a spirit of self-sacrifice, all of which contribute to mutuality and all of which can be adopted by others.

The second objection I occasionally receive is the complaint, 'What right have you to impose your views about mutuality on social welfare?' The advocates of mutuality cannot impose anything. We tend to lack money, power, access to the media. What influence we do have is minute compared with the New Right. None the less, we do want to promote personal social services in a different mould. I do not expect this challenge and alternative to the policies of the New Right to be accepted with the no-arguing, no-compromising blindness of the 'No Turning Back' school. However I do firmly believe that services built on the concept of mutuality will lead not only to a more humane, more just and more altruistic welfare but also to a more efficient and more democratic one. Let this be debated.

Inevitably, the objection of costs is made. Alvin Schorr estimates that the personal social services are already £500 million under-financed. I am not in a position to assess accurately the costs of the proposed switch to community social work, additional family centres and increased funding of community groups, but it would certainly be in this range.

Yet the priority given to prevention would also produce savings. A study made in just one London borough showed that keeping children out of public care could save £1.3 million a year.[100] Further, the expansion of jobs associated with the emphasis on family centres and community groups would occur in areas of high unemployment, so saving the state considerable amounts of money spent on benefits. The employed people's increased income would be spent locally, so boosting run-down economies. This could contribute to what could be a much wider strategy, as argued by Will Hutton, of promoting economic revival by increasing the purchasing power of poor people. As he states, 'The fight against poverty is not merely a moral injunction: the just society begets the sound economy.'[101] Money spent on the personal social services is not a bottomless pit, it is a sound investment.

But despite the much-publicized government budget deficit, it should also be made clear that Britain is not short of resources. It contains 95,000 millionaires, much of whose wealth derives not from productive work but from inheritance. One recently left £85 million to his already wealthy heirs. It is a society which can afford an economic system which, on Black Wednesday 1992, allows speculators to take £5 billion out of the economy. If the Government wants money it produces it. It directed £8 billion to a quango, the London Docklands

Development Corporation, much of which went to profit private building companies. The same Government in 1993 announced a £23 billion road-building project, with the lion's share going to the already prosperous south-east. Its budgets have awarded huge tax relief to private pensions while tax and benefit changes between 1979 and 1989 diverted £8 billion from poor to affluent citizens.

Undoubtedly Britain requires a productive economy. But the problem is not just the amount of resources but how they are distributed. During the war, when I was an evacuee, food became more scarce for the nation. Yet, because of more equal distribution, the health of working-class children actually improved. Today the nation possesses vast resources but lacks the political will to share them fairly. Thus in 1989 the poorer half of the population had only 27 per cent of all income (after housing costs) while the richer half had 73 per cent. Indeed, if the income tax paid by those earning over £50,000 was raised by 20 per cent, they would still have high incomes while the country would gain an extra £4–5 billion. In terms of wealth, in 1990 a mere 10 per cent of the population owned over 50 per cent of the national marketable wealth of £1,700 billion. These inequalities have been widened by the policies of the New Right. By contrast, policies based on the values of mutuality could redistribute goods to promote greater equality and to make more available to the personal social services. Our kin would then share the advantages enjoyed by others.

Now

I have been involved with the personal social services for over three decades. In recent years I have witnessed them undergo changes under the influence of New Right doctrines and policies. In the first half of this book, I attempted to identify the limitations and dangers of these changes. In their place, I put forward the concept of mutuality as a foundation on which to build an alternative. The kind of services I envisage will require a government willing to redistribute income, wealth and power radically. They will require local authorities willing to develop agencies which emphasize support, prevention and participation. They will require staff who hold the values and objectives associated with mutuality. Central and local government policies are shaped by public opinion and propagation. I hope these words are a small contribution towards winning minds and hearts.

I write in 1993, soon after the implementation of the Community Care Act (1990). The personal social services are still changing. My fears and hopes have been highlighted in two incidents. I saw a letter from a member of MENCAP to a social work magazine. She wrote:

'Recently I attended a workshop on purchasing services for people with a learning difficulty. I was dismayed to hear from professionals that carers should not be consulted or involved in planning services; the argument being carers could "vote with their feet" if they did not like the set-up. This implies, as in the case of a supermarket, there is a variety of alternative choices. Exactly who would be "voting with their feet"? A person with a learning difficulty who is unable to communicate with no advocate? A harassed mother seeking respite care? A frail elderly person seeking residential care for a son or daughter? We should not be seduced by the idea there will be much choice in services for learning difficulties.'[102]

The writer reflects my fear that the personal social services are in danger of becoming like private business enterprises in which staff no longer act as social workers who empathize with users and advocate on their behalf, but as salespersons who supply goods on a 'take it or leave it' basis. And if the goods don't suit, too bad, go away.

The other incident occurred when I stopped my van in Easterhouse to watch an eviction. A young woman stood on the pavement with her baby in her arms, surrounded by her meagre possessions. She had been slung out not by the authorities but by neighbours who alleged that she was continuously having young people in for sex and drugs. In fact the authorities declined to come, apparently on the grounds that the woman was a squatter. A passing woman stopped and then invited her home. I loaded the van and we all drove to her flat. In reply to my questions, this Good Samaritan said she did not know the girl but that she too was a lone parent who had been through hard times. Here was a sharing of goods and a giving of self based on a recognition of a common tie—mutuality.

It is fitting to end with this example of mutuality being expressed by the kind of person who might be a user of the personal social services. For I believe our society suffers from a top down approach in which powerful elites impose their views, explanations and policies on those from whom they keep a geographical and social distance, on those whose behaviour they do not understand, on those from whom they should learn. Yet here was an Income Support recipient, dwelling in a council flat, displaying the kind of mutuality which, hopefully, will permeate upwards to influence the nature of social welfare. Further—and unlike those intellectuals who proclaim lofty principles and then refrain from applying them until some distant future—the woman applied her beliefs immediately.

If we are to have personal social services based on the values of mutuality, then we must begin practising it now.

References

CHAPTER 1

1. M. Friedman, *Capitalism and Freedom*, University of Chicago Press, 1962, page 6.

2. *Idem*, pages 2–3.

3. *Idem*, page 174.

4. Cited by M. Bayley, *Welfare: A Moral Issue*, Diocese of Sheffield Social Responsibility Committee, 1989, page 45.

5. M. Friedman, *op. cit.*, page 5.

6. *Idem*, page 188.

7. *Idem*, page 189.

8. A. Seldon, 'Welfare By Choice', in A. Lochhead (ed.), *A Reader In Social Administration*, Constable, 1968, page 264.

9. M. Friedman, *op. cit.*, page 195.

10. *Idem*, page 190.

11. *Idem*, page 33.

12. C. Murray, *The Emerging British Underclass*, Institute of Economic Affairs, 1990, page 17.

13. M. Parris, *The Times*, 29 September 1992.

14. R. Dahrendorf, 'Footnotes to the Discussion', in D. Smith (ed.), *Understanding the Underclass*, Policy Studies Institute, 1992, page 59.

15. D. Anderson, *Sunday Times*, 30 September 1990.

16. C. Murray, *op. cit.*, page 72.

17. C. Murray, *op. cit.*, page 12.

18. M. Friedman, *op. cit.*, page 3.

19. A. Heath, 'The Attitudes of the Underclass', in D. Smith, *op. cit.*, chapter 3.

20. K. Mann, *The Making of an English Underclass*, Oxford University Press, 1992, page 107.

21. M. Friedman, *op. cit.*, page 199.

22. *Idem*, page 109.

23. F. Hayek, *The Road to Serfdom*, Routledge & Kegan Paul, 1944.

24. R. Titmuss, 'The Irresponsible Society', reprinted in R. Titmuss, *Essays On The 'Welfare State'*, Unwin University Books, 2nd edition, 1963, page 243.

25. M. Schluter and D. Lee, *The R Factor*, Hodder & Stoughton, 1993, pages 172–3.

CHAPTER 2

26. National Institute of Social Work, *Social Workers: Their Role and Tasks* (Barclay Report), Bedford Square Press, 1982, paras 10 and 1.2.

27. *Caring For People*, HMSO, 1989, paras 1.8, 1.11.

28. Cited by T. Philpot, 'The Other Man'. *Community Care*, 1 October 1992.

29. T. Hunter, 'A Vision of the Next Five Years', *Community Care*, 6 February 1992.

30. D. Donnison and V. Chapman, *Social Policy and Administration Re-Visited*, Allen & Unwin, 1975.

31. D. Platt, 'After the New Dawn—What Next?', *Community Care*, 12 March 1992.

32. Cited by N. Murray, 'Contract for Care', *Community Care*, 6 September 1992.

33. R. Gutch, 'A Mission to Survive', *Community Care*, 28 January 1993.

34. Disablement Income Group, *Evidence to Social Services Committee of The House of Commons*, May 1990.

35. Cited by D. Clode, 'A New Wave Manager', *Community Care*, 15 October 1992.

36. A. Schorr, *The Personal Social Services: An Outsider's View*, Rowntree Foundation, 1992, page 45.

37. N. Parton, *The Politics of Child Abuse*, Macmillan, 1985.

38. A. Schorr, *op. cit.*, page 33.

39. *Idem.*

40. B. Jordan, *Social Work in an Unjust Society*, Harvester Wheatsheaf, 1990, page 3.

41. D. Platt, 'The Age of Mutual Consent', *Community Care*, 22 April 1993.

42. A. Schorr, *op. cit.*, page 27.

43. J. Gibbons with S. Thorpe and P. Wilkinson, *Family Support and Prevention*, HMSO, 1990, page 51.

44. *Supporting Families: Preventative Social Work in Practice*, National Children's Bureau, 1992.

45. B. Holman, 'Keeping Children Out of Care', *The Guardian*, 12 April 1989.

46. *The Report of the Committee on Local Authority and Allied Personal Social Services*, (Seebohm Report), HMSO, 1968, and National Institute of Social Work (Barclay Report), *op. cit.*

47. K. Ellis, *Squaring the Circle*, Rowntree Foundation, 1993.

48. Public Services Privatization Research Unit, *Community Care Policies of Local Authorities and Boards*, 1993.

49. D. Clode, 'The Profit Speaks', *Community Care*, 17 September 1992.

50. A. Kestenbaum, *Taking Care in the Market: A Study of Agency Homecare*, Independent Living Fund, 1993.

51. L. Fox Harding, *Perspectives in Child Care Policy*, Longman, 1991.

52. Cited in *The Guardian*, 5 December 1992.

53. J. Gibbons, *op. cit.*, page 159.

54. Cited in *Community Care*, 16 May 1990.

55. Cited in *Community Care*, 22 April 1993.

56. J. Findlay, 'Taken to the Limit', *Social Work Today*, 14 January 1993.

57. G. Clapton, 'A Badge Too Far', *Social Work Today*, 25 June 1992.

58. H. Lamming, 'Shifting Power', *Social Work Today*, 1 October 1992.

59. B. Hughes, 'Finance and Management', *Community Care*, 25 February 1993.

CHAPTER 3

60. F. Biestek, *The Casework Relationship*, Allen & Unwin, 1961.

61. N. Biehal, in A. Coote (ed.), *The Welfare of Citizens*, Rivers Oram Press, 1992.

62. E. Hobsbawm, 'Fraternity', *New Society*, 27 November 1975.

63. R. Terrill, *R. H. Tawney and his Times*, Deutsch, 1973, page 218.

64. Cited by E. Thompson, *William Morris*, Merlin, 1977, page 129.

65. R.Tawney, *The Attack and Other Papers*, Spokesman, 1987, page 60.

66. G. Lansbury, *My Life*, Constable, 1928, page 265.

67. G. Carey, *The Gate of Glory*, Hodder & Stoughton, 1992, page 179.

68. Philippians 2:4; 2 Corinthians 8:14, Good News Bible.

69. R. Lister, *The Exclusive Society: Citizenship and the Poor*, Child Poverty Action Group, 1990.

CHAPTER 4

70. R. Terrill, *op. cit.*, page 218.

71. *Contracts at the Crossroads*, Association of Crossroads Care Attendance Schemes, 1991.

72. *Swept under the Carpet*, Age Concern, 1992.

73. See, J. Heywood, *Children in Care*, Routledge & Kegan Paul, 1959, page 165.

74. Cited in *Community Care*, 25 February 1993.

75. A. Schorr, *op. cit.*, page 40.

76. Cited in *Community Care*, 14 January 1993.

77. L. Hoyes and R. Mearns, 'Making Changes', *Community Care*, 20 May 1993.

CHAPTER 5

78. Cited in *Social Work Today*, 19 September 1992.

79. A. Schorr, *op. cit.*, page 41.

80. C. Cannan, *Changing Families: Changing Welfare*, Harvester Wheatsheaf, 1992, pages 144–49.

81. J. Gibbons, *op. cit.*, page 148.

82. National Institute of Social Work (Barclay Report), *op. cit.*, para. 23.

83. See, B. Holman, 'Pulling Together', *The Guardian*, 20 January 1993.

84. S. Rogowski, 'Streetwise', *Social Work Today*, 27 June 1991.

85. M. Bayley, R. Seyd and A. Tennant, *Local Health and Welfare, Is Partnership Possible?*, Gower, 1989.

86. C. Warren, *The Potential for Family Advocacy in Family Centres*, M.Phil. Thesis, University of Southampton, 1991.

87. C. Cannan, *op. cit.*, page 105.

88. J. Gibbons, *op. cit.*, page 130.

CHAPTER 6

89. *Idem*, page 158.

90. B. Holman, *Putting Families First*, Macmillan, 1988, chapter 6.

91. C. Cannan, *op. cit.*, page 126.

92. B. Holman, *op. cit.*, chapter 6.

93. J. Gibbons, *op. cit.*, page 121.

94. *Idem.* page 148.

95. R. Fowles, 'Preventing Reception into Care: Monitoring an Initiative Using Section 12 Funding', in I. Freeman and S. Montgomery (eds), *Research Highlights in Social Work 17: Child Care Monitoring Practice*, Jessica Kingsley, 1988.

96. Cited by B. Holman, *Good Old George: The Life of George Lansbury*, Lion, 1990, page 174. For Will Crooks, who spent part of his childhood in the workhouse, see G. Haw, *From Workhouse to Westminster*, Cassell, 1907.

97. C. Murray, *op. cit.*, page 12.

98. J. Gibbons, *op. cit.*, page 162.

CHAPTER 7

99. A. Phillips, 'Fraternity' in B. Pimlott (ed.), *Fabian Essays In Socialist Thought*, Heinemann, 1984.

100. See B. Holman, *Putting Families First*, op. cit., page 89.

101. W. Hutton, 'The Real Price Of Poverty', *The Guardian*, 24 February 1992.

102. Community Care, 4 March 1993.

By the same author:

Good Old George
The life of George Lansbury
Best-loved leader of the Labour Party

Bob Holman

George Lansbury led the Labour Party in the crisis
years of the early 1930s. Throughout that time, he
campaigned with passionate sincerity for a just society.
He was a working man, and he spoke his message of
social justice in words that ordinary people could
understand. He sought practical ways to relieve
poverty.

His sincerity and commitment to the cause of social
justice have made him what the historian A.J.P. Taylor
has described as 'the most loveable figure in modern
politics'. But Lansbury himself would probably have
appreciated more the chants of children whenever he
appeared at schools or in playgrounds: 'Good old
George.'

ISBN 0 7459 1574 4

Making Unemployment Work

Dr Michael Moynagh

This book is about the people who are hidden behind the unemployment statistics. What does it feel like to be put on the dole queue and to become one of the long-term unemployed? How does it feel for a teenager who has never had a job and whose mates are all in the same boat? Why are so many people out of work—and what can be done about it?

Some people feel that unemployment, like the weather, is simply a fact of life. There is nothing we can do about it. This book disagrees. It points to positive but realistic ways forward for individual people, local groups and for national policy.

ISBN 0 85648 849 6

A selection of top titles from LION PUBLISHING:

GOOD OLD GEORGE Bob Holman   £5.99☐
MAKING UNEMPLOYMENT WORK
Michael Moynagh   £3.95☐
WHO PROFITS? Richard Adams   £4.99☐
KILLING TIME Noel Fellowes   £4.99☐
MUMMY, WHY HAVE I GOT DOWN'S SYNDROME?
Caroline Philps   £4.99☐
CANCER HELP Marion Stroud   £5.99☐
ALZHEIMER'S Sharon Fish   £7.99☐
BEREAVEMENT: A SHARED EXPERIENCE
Helen Alexander   £5.99☐
CLIMBING OUT OF DEPRESSION
Sue Atkinson   £4.99☐

All Lion paperbacks are available from your local bookshop or newsagent, or can be ordered direct from the address below. Just tick the titles you want and fill in the form.

Name (Block letters)

Address _____

_____

_____

Write to Lion Publishing, Cash Sales Department, PO Box 11, Falmouth, Cornwall TR10 9EN, England.

Please enclose a cheque or postal order to the value of the cover price plus:

UK INCLUDING BFPO: £1.00 for the first book, 50p for the second book and 30p for each additional book ordered to a maximum charge of £3.00.

OVERSEAS INCLUDING EIRE: £2.00 for the first book, £1.00 for the second book and 50p for each additional book.

Lion Publishing reserves the right to show on covers and charge new retail prices which may differ from those previously advertised in the text or elsewhere, and to increase postal rates in accordance with the Post Office.